www.icehockeyreview.co.uk

UK Hockey Yearbook 2017

THE 2016/17 SEASON
Covering
EIHL, EPL, NIHL North & South, SNL
WEL, WPL, WD1N&S and Para Ice Hockey

With a foreword by Stewart Roberts

Interesting Books...
...Fascinating Subjects!

www.poshupnorth.com

ISBN: 978-1-909643-20-8

First published in Great Britain in October 2017 by
Posh Up North Publishing
c/o 2 Beckenham Road, New Brighton CH45 2NZ

British Library cataloguing in publication data.
A catalogue record for this book is available from the British Library

Front Cover Photo:
Solway Sharks v Solihull Barons in the NIHL North Moralee Conference Play Off Semi Final
(Photo by Duncan Speirs)

Back Cover Photos:

Left Column - Top to Bottom:	Right Column – Top to Bottom:
Cardiff Devils by Helen Brabon	Braehead Clan by Al Goold
Telford Tigers by Steve Brodie	Milton Keynes Lightning by Lucy McGill
Solway Sharks by Duncan Speirs	Chelmsford Chieftains by Steve Sutherland
Blackburn Eagles by Ella Thornton	Peterborough Islanders by Tom Scott
Solihull Vixens by My Team Photo	Paisley Pirates by Al Goold
Streatham Storm by Storm IHC	

Statistics are taken from a variety of sources, including the EIHA website, Fixtures Live, www.malcolm preen.co.uk and www.thesnl.co.uk. Particular thanks to Kevin Garrad, EIHA Chief Statistician

Big thanks to all the team officials and reporters who took the time to send in their season reports. Each author and photographer is acknowledged on their individual submissions.

As ever – if YOUR team isn't covered in the way you would have liked to see, it is probably because they didn't provide the information when invited to do so!

CONTENTS

FOREWORD
BY STEWART ROBERTS

You didn't expect to see me here, eh? Frankly, neither did I, but editor Paul kindly asked me to say a few words and I couldn't resist the offer.

First, it gives me a chance to say farewell to at least some of the readers of The Ice Hockey Annual which, after 40 years and 41 editions, I have decided to give up.

Second, I hope many readers of the Annual will be persuaded to switch to reading Ice Hockey Review in future as it will be covering all the former English Premier League (EPIHL) clubs that have joined the National League (NIHL).

Now I realise that this move was not necessarily good news for some EPIHL fans who are upset at their team 'dropping down' a level from season 2017-18, or indeed for many NIHL clubs who are concerned about the competition. But I believe it's a sensible decision by the sport's authorities who, as many of you know, I have not always been a big fan of in the past.

If you read the EPIHL clubs' reports in these pages, you will understand that, as always, money is the sole reason for this change. The teams simply could not afford the standard of hockey they were trying to operate.

The shenanigans that had been going on at the Phoenix for so long were only the most obvious example of the financial straits that many clubs were in (and what a shame that Tony Hand MBE became mixed up with the Phoenix).

Telford Tigers' league success will always be tarnished by the collapse of their ownership group in mid-season. The upside is that this shouldn't happen again - the NIHL have shrewdly added some new rules designed to punish clubs that get themselves into this situation. (And hopefully, we will never again have to listen to Wayne Scholes's unwanted advice!)

Personally, I think Tigers' coach Tom Watkins deserves some kind of medal for keeping the ship afloat in the midst of all the background noise.

I sincerely hope the old teams mix well with the new ones in the expanded NIHL as the sport will benefit from having a stable second tier, even if the gap between it and the Elite League is too wide for developing our local players successfully.

Unfortunately, I guess many youngsters, or at least those lucky enough to have parents with deep pockets, will still opt to go abroad to further their hockey education.

Not all the EPIHL teams were mismanaged, of course. In fact, two of the better ones have joined the Elite League - Milton Keynes Lightning and my local side Guildford Flames. This will be a suck-it-and-see season for both of them and I wish them the best of luck.

Thanks again to Paul for giving me this space and for insisting I remind you that back issues of The Ice Hockey Annual are always available via our website at

www.icehockeyannual.co.uk.

Cardiff Devils won the 2016/17 Erhardt Conference and overall Elite League titles as well as the 2017 EIHL Challenge Cup
(Photo by Helen Brabon – www.helenbrabonphotography.co.uk)

Braehead Clan celebrate winning the Gardiner Conference title.
Photo by Al Goold Photography (www.algooldphoto.com)

Back Row (players l-r): Mike Hammond; Stefan Della Rovere; Kyle Wharton; Cody Carlson; Daniel Ahsberg; Callum Boyd; Lee Baldwin; Corey Cowick; Zach Sullivan; Craig Peacock; Gary Russell; Scott Aarssen:
Front Row (players l-r): Matt Haywood; Matt Beca; Scott Pitt; Matt Keith; Alex Leavitt; Bari McKenzie; Jay Rosehill; Michal Zajkowski

Elite League

Braehead Clan's Matt Beca (above left) was the Elite League's top scorer. (Photo by Al Goold)
Ben Bowns of Cardiff Devils (above right) was the top overall netminder (Photo by Helen Brabon).

Mathieu Roy (above left) and Ervīns Muštukovs (above right) were the highest rated points scorer and netminder respectively from the Erhardt Conference. (Photos by Dean Woolley Photography).

Dean Woolley Photography
www.deanwoolley.co.uk

Elite League Final League Tables 2016/17

Elite League (Overall)	GP	W	OW	OL	L	F	A	Pts
Cardiff Devils	52	32	7	3	10	200	136	81
Belfast Giants	52	30	5	4	13	195	145	74
Sheffield Steelers	52	31	4	3	14	196	136	73
Nottingham Panthers	52	22	4	6	20	169	175	58
Braehead Clan	52	24	3	3	22	191	176	57
Fife Flyers	52	19	6	3	24	174	186	53
Dundee Stars	52	16	4	7	25	162	183	47
Manchester Storm	52	17	1	8	26	141	168	44
Coventry Blaze	52	13	6	5	28	147	198	43
Edinburgh Capitals	52	11	5	3	33	154	226	35

Erhardt Conference	GP	W	OW	OL	L	F	A	Pts
Cardiff Devils	32	18	3	3	8	119	96	45
Belfast Giants	32	16	4	2	10	104	88	42
Sheffield Steelers	32	17	1	2	12	121	88	38
Nottingham Panthers	32	11	2	4	15	104	119	30
Coventry Blaze	32	4	4	3	21	84	141	19

Gardiner Conference	GP	W	OW	OL	L	F	A	Pts
Braehead Clan	32	22	1	1	8	136	97	47
Dundee Stars	32	14	3	4	11	117	106	38
Fife Flyers	32	12	2	3	15	117	121	31
Manchester Storm	32	12	1	3	16	93	101	29
Edinburgh Capitals	32	8	5	1	18	101	139	27

Top Points Scorers (Overall) – Season 2016/17

Player	Team	GP	G	A	Pts	PIM
Matt Beca	Braehead Clan	52	27	48	75	28
Scott Pitt	Braehead Clan	52	32	42	74	26
Vinny Scarsella	Dundee Stars	52	18	54	72	4
Alex Leavitt	Braehead Clan	52	24	45	69	57
Mathieu Roy	Sheffield Steelers	52	28	29	57	28
Blair Riley	Belfast Giants	52	28	28	56	77
Chris Higgins	Belfast Giants	49	20	35	55	107
Mathew Sisca	Fife Flyers	50	17	38	55	44
Ryan Dingle	Fife Flyers	41	31	23	54	32
Kevin Bruijsten	Dundee Stars	47	23	31	54	10

Leading Netminders (Overall) - Season 2016/17

Player	Team	GP	TOI	GA	SO	SV%	GAA
Ben Bowns	Cardiff Devils	46	2616:43	103	3	0.912	2.36
Ervīns Muštukovs	Sheffield Steelers	51	3053:14	130	1	0.913	2.55
Stephen Murphy	Belfast Giants	39	2284:16	97	3	0.905	2.55
Mike Clemente	Manchester Storm	52	3108:38	150	3	0.91	2.9
Miika Wiikman	Nottingham Panthers	41	2294:47	115	2	0.901	3.01

Elite League

Sheffield Steelers celebrate their play-off final victory over Cardiff Devils (Photo by Dean Woolley)

EIHL Play Off Final (at NIC, Nottingham)
Sunday, 9th April, 2017
Cardiff Devils 5 – Sheffield Steelers 6 (OTW)
Period Scores: 3-1, 1-4, 1-0, 0-0, 0-1
Shots on Goal: Devils 40 – Steelers 51
Penalties In Minutes: Devils 6 – Steelers 10

Scoring Summary:

Period 1:
Cardiff Devils - Guillaume Doucet (power play) (Andrew Hotham, Scott Hotham) 2:20
Sheffield Steelers - John Armstrong (unassisted) 3:52
Cardiff Devils - Joey Haddad (Patrick Asselin) 16:10
Cardiff Devils - Joey Martin (power play) (Andrew Hotham, Andrew Lord) 19:17

Period 2:
Sheffield Steelers - Geoff Walker (Ben O Connor) 4:24
Sheffield Steelers - Colton Fretter (Luke Ferrara, Cole Shudra) 5:54
Sheffield Steelers - Levi Nelson (power play) (Mathieu Roy, Ben O Connor) 8:45
Cardiff Devils - Layne Ulmer (Joey Haddad) 12:20
Sheffield Steelers - Geoff Walker (Markus Nilsson) 17:23

Period 3:
Cardiff Devils - Andrew Hotham (power play) (unassisted) 0:54

1st Overtime: (no scoring)
2nd Overtime: Sheffield Steelers - Levi Nelson (unassisted) 14:08

Match Officials:
Referee: Toby Craig
Referee 2: Dean Smith
Linesman 1: Allan Ward
Linesman 2: James Kavanagh

Cardiff Devils
Full Lineup:
Louis,Mark
Myers, Matthew
Brine, David
Doucet, Guillaume
Jones, Chris
Richardson, Mark
Ulmer, Layne
Fournier, Gleason
Piggott, Luke
Kearney, Denny
Asselin, Patrick
Hotham, Andrew
Haddad, Joey
Murdy, Thomas
Bowns, Ben
Batch, Josh
Culligan, Chris
Bordeleau, Patrick
Lord, Andrew
Hotham, Scott
Bentivoglio, Sean
Martin, Joey

Sheffield Steelers
Full Lineup:
Franzon, Anders
Valdix, Andreas
Phillips, David
Roy, Mathieu
Nilsson, Markus
Ferrara, Luke
Phillips, Jonathan
Coyle, Jace
Shudra, Cole
Fitzgerald, Zack
Sarich, Rodney
Day, Brad
Mustukovs, Ervins
Desbiens, Guillaume
Fretter, Colton
Walker, Geoff
Dowd, Robert
Nelson, Levi
O Connor, Ben
Armstrong, John
Hagos, Yared

Bronze Medal Game (at NIC, Nottingham)
Sunday, 9th April, 2017
Dundee Stars 8 – Belfast Giants 15
Period Scores: 4-4, 2-5, 2-6

Elite League

Elite League Play Offs – Semi Finals
Played at National Ice Centre Nottingham, Saturday 8th April 2017

1st Semi Final
Cardiff Devils 4 - Dundee Stars 2
Period Scores: 0-2, 1-0, 3-0
Shots on Goal: Devils 38 – Stars 26
Penalties In Minutes: Devils 2 – Stars 2

2nd Semi Final
Belfast Giants 0 – Sheffield Steelers 2
Period Scores: 0-1, 0-0, 0-1
Shots on Goal: Giants 31 – Steelers 18
Penalties In Minutes: Giants 6 – Steelers 2

Elite League Play Offs – Quarter Finals

1st Leg - 1st April 2017	2nd Leg - 2nd April 2017	Aggregate Score
Cardiff Devils 3 - Manchester Storm 2	Manchester Storm 1 – Cardiff Devils 3	Cardiff win 6-3
Dundee Stars 3- Braehead Clan 1	Braehead Clan 0- Dundee Stars 3	Stars win 6-1
Nott'm Panthers 5 – Sheffield Steelers 2	Sheff Steelers 4 – Nott'm Panthers 1	Steelers win 7-6 OTW
Belfast Giants 4 - Fife Flyers 2	Fife Flyers 1- Belfast Giants 4	Giants win 8-3

ELITE LEAGUE CHALLENGE CUP

Elite League Challenge Cup Final
(Played at Ice Arena Wales, Cardiff)
Sunday, 5th March 2017
Sheffield Steelers 2 - Cardiff Devils 3
Period Scores: 2-1, 0-1, 0-1

Elite League Challenge Cup – Semi Finals

1st Leg	2nd Leg	Aggregate Score
Notting'm Panthers 1 - Sheffield Steelers 2	Sheff Steelers 3 – Nottm Panthers 0	Steelers win 5-1
Cardiff Devils 4 – Belfast Giants 5	Belfast Giants 1 - Cardiff Devils 5	Devils win 9-6

Elite League Challenge Cup – Quarter Finals

1st Leg	2nd Leg	Aggregate Score
Edinburgh Capitals 2 Sheffield Steelers 2	Sheff Steelers 7 – Edinburgh Caps 1	Steelers win 9-3
Dundee Stars 1- Cardiff Devils 4	Cardiff Devils 4 - Dundee Stars 2	Devils win 8-3
Braehead Clan 3 - Nott'm Panthers 3	Nott'm Panthers 3 – Breahead Clan 1	Panthers win 6-4
Manchester Storm 3 - Belfast Giants3	Belfast Giants 4 – Storm 3	Giants win 7-6

Elite League Challenge Cup – Group Stage

Group A	Pts
Belfast Giants	13
Dundee Stars	11
Braehead Clan	9
Edinburgh Capitals	8
Fife Flyers	5

Group B	Pts
Nottingham Panthers	12
Sheffield Steelers	12
Cardiff Devils	8
Manchester Storm	6
Coventry Blaze	5

English Premier League

Telford Tigers captain Jason Silverthorn receives the EPL league trophy from EIHA Chairman Ken Taggart

(Photo by Steve Brodie / Tigers Photos)

Hull Pirates' Andrej Themar was the EPL's top points scorer. (Photo by Lois Tomlinson)

MK Lightning's Przemyslaw Odrobny was top netminder (Photo by Lucy McGill Photography)

EPL Final League Table – Season 2016/17

Team	P	W	OW	OL	L	PIM	GF	GA	Pts
Telford Tigers	48	33	7	3	5	737	220	128	83
Milton Keynes Lightning	48	28	6	3	11	856	174	124	71
Basingstoke Bison	48	29	1	1	17	940	169	112	61
Peterborough Phantoms	48	27	2	2	17	575	186	141	60
Guildford Flames	48	20	2	5	21	905	176	171	49
Swindon Wildcats	48	14	8	4	22	816	156	170	48
Hull Pirates	48	20	0	2	26	878	162	201	42
Sheffield Steeldogs	48	9	2	6	31	1068	153	225	28
Bracknell Bees	48	6	2	4	36	804	113	237	20
Manchester Phoenix	*38*	*4*	*2*	*1*	*31*	*305*	*91*	*219*	*13*

Manchester Phoenix withdrew from the league on 30th January 2017 and all previous results for the season were expunged from the records. For the sake of completeness, their playing record up to that date is shown above but is not included in the rest of the final league table.

EPL Top Points Scorers – Season 2016/17

Player	Team	GP	G	A	Pts	PIM
Andrej Themar	Hull Pirates	45	46	36	82	42
Matthew Davies	Telford Tigers	42	16	63	79	54
Arnoldas Bosas	Sheffield Steeldogs	47	34	44	78	67
Tomasz Malasinski	Swindon Wildcats	46	36	39	75	44
Doug Clarkson	Telford Tigers	46	43	30	73	96
Jonas Hoog	Swindon Wildcats	48	17	56	73	20
Ciaran Long	Basingstoke Bison	47	33	30	63	80
Stanislav Lascek	Hull Pirates	28	23	39	62	72
Stanislav Lascek	Sheffield Steeldogs	11	23	39	62	72
Jason Silverthorn	Telford Tigers	45	37	24	61	51
Ben Campbell	Guildford Flames	45	30	30	60	20

EPL Top Netminders – Season 2016/17

Netminder	Team	GP	SA	GA	Sv%	SO
Przemyslaw Odrobny	Milton Keynes	47	1559	111	92.88%	3
Janis Auzins	Peterborough	37	1125	82	92.71%	6
Jon Baston	Telford Tigers	19	276	22	92.03%	1
Ondrej Raszka	Telford Tigers	22	459	38	91.72%	1
Tomas Hiadlovsky	Basingstoke	48	1235	106	91.42%	4
Jordan Marr	Hull Pirates	31	1010	88	91.29%	2
Samuel Gospel	Telford Tigers	46	694	64	90.78%	0
Stevie Lyle	Swindon Wildcats	48	1681	160	90.48%	1
Mike Will	Guildford Flames	42	300	30	90.00%	2
Dean Skinns	Guildford Flames	31	690	74	89.28%	2

English Premier League

BASINGSTOKE BISON
Top Three Again
By GRAHAM MERRY *Basingstoke Gazette*

Trying to retain their English Premier League crown was always going to be hard for the Bison and so it proved.

The season began with high scoring imports **Tomas Karpov** and **Rene Jarolin** back in the line-up, and they were joined by Czech pair, forward **Petr Polodna** and defenceman **Jakub Barton**. On the British side of the roster **Lewis Turner** and **Ivan Antonov** came from Bracknell, along with **Dan Davies** from Telford.

Though the team looked strong on paper they got off to an awful start, winning just once in their first six league games. Coach **Doug Sheppard** changed his imports, releasing the Czechs and introducing Italian-American forward **Derek Roehl** from the Elite League and Slovak defenceman **Jan Jarabek**.

The upheaval was worth it as it produced the Bison's best winning streak of the season with seven straight in October. After this only Guildford Flames and Telford Tigers escaped from the Basingstoke Arena with two wins.

There were more changes in December when forward **Shaun Thompson** left for neighbours Bracknell and Jarabek was released. In their stead, Sheppard snapped up Telford's defenceman **Dan Scott** and forward **Joe Miller**, while popular Canadian **Joe Rand** returned to give the side four import forwards.

The bad start to the campaign came back to haunt the Herd in the Cup as they failed to make the final four. And they had to settle for third place in the league, though this maintained Sheppard's impressive run of a top three finish throughout his tenure.

The Bison topped their Play-off group with only one defeat in six games and went on to outshoot the league-winning Tigers in the semi-final. But they conceded a powerplay goal early in the last period and lost 3-2.

PLAYER AWARDS
Players' Player (Mark Scotchmer Award):
Ciaran Long
Player of the Year: **Rene Jarolin**
Coach's Player: **Matt Towalski**
British Player of the Year: **Ciaran Long**

FACT FILE 2016-17
English Premier League: Third
Play-offs: Semi-finalists
Premier Cup: Fifth in first round

LEADING PLAYERS
Ivan Antonov *born 12 May 1997, Moscow*
The GB under-20's agility, speed and pin-point passing make him a joy to watch.
René Jarolin *born 16 September 1981, Slovakia*
In his first full season with the club he shone with some brilliant goals and was also an excellent playmaker.
Ciaran Long *born 9 February 1991, Birmingham*
The team's all-time top goal and points scorer possesses a superb shot, which is especially lethal from the point on the powerplay.

Tomas Hiadlovsky set a new and unusual club record with six assists, the most in a season by a netminder. It would have been seven, but the one against the Phoenix was wiped from the records

HISTORY: Founded 1988 as Beavers. Name changed to Bison in May 1995.
Leagues English (Premier) League 2009-17, 198890; Elite League 2003-09; British National League 1998-2003; Superleague 1996-98; British League, Premier Div 1993-96; BL Div One 1990-93.
Honours: English Premier League 2015-16; EPL Play-offs 2013-14; Premier Cup 2013-14; British League, Div One & play-offs 1992-93; English League (promotion) play-offs 1989-90; *Benson and Hedges* Plate 1999-2000 & 2000-01.

BASINGSTOKE BISON – PLAYER STATISTICS 2016/17

Scorers	LEAGUE					PLAY OFFS				
	GP	G	A	Pts	Pim	GP	G	A	Pts	Pim
Ciaran Long	47	33	30	63	80	7	4	3	7	8
Rene Jarolin (I)	48	23	31	54	18	7	1	5	6	2
Derek Roehl (I)	41	18	19	37	121	7	5	7	12	14
Tomas Karpov (I)	47	17	26	43	22	7	3	3	6	2
Shaun Thompson 2	20	8	4	12	14					
Ivan Antonov	38	15	18	33	16	6	2	4	6	0
Dan Davies	47	8	27	35	14	7	0	4	4	0
Aaron Connolly	45	13	13	26	51	7	5	2	7	25
Declan Balmer	47	2	20	22	150	7	0	5	5	4
Kurt Reynolds	47	1	17	18	74	7	0	1	1	12
Joe Miller 1	17	3	5	8	22	7	5	5	10	4
Matt Towalski	45	9	7	16	77	7	0	1	1	0
Joe Baird	43	1	11	12	80	7	0	5	5	4
Stuart Mogg	45	3	11	14	16	7	0	0	0	0
Joe Rand	21	5	3	8	40	7	2	1	3	6
Jan Jarabek (I)	20	2	9	11	12					
Grant Rounding	48	4	5	9	16	6	0	0	0	0
Tomas Hiadlovsky (N) (I)	48	0	6	6	45	7	0	0	0	2
Dan Scott 1	19	1	1	2	28	7	2	1	3	8
Dan Lackey	47	2	3	5	20	7	0	0	0	0
Petr Polodna (I)	6	0	3	3	0					
Alan Lack	11	1	1	2	14					
Jakub Barton	5	0	0	0	4					
Winning shots		0		0			0		0	
Bench penalties					10					2
TEAM TOTALS	**48**	**169**	**270**	**439**	**944**	**7**	**29**	**47**	**76**	**93**

Netminders	LEAGUE					PLAY OFFS				
	GPI	Mins	SOG	GA	Sv%	GPI	Mins	SOG	GA	Sv%
Tomas Hiadlovsky i	48	2841	1235	106	92.1	7	412	158	14	91.1
Dan Weller-Evans	4	40	22	3	88	1	6	3	1	66.7
Winning shots				1					0	
Empty net goals			2	2						
TEAM TOTALS		**2881**	**1259**	**112**	**91.1**	**7**	**418**	**161**	**15**	**90.7**

Also appeared: *Kyle Goddard, Lewis Turner, Paul Petts.*

Also played for: *1 Telford Tigers; 2 Bracknell Bees.*

Shutouts: *Hiadlovsky (5) - league: 1 Oct v Sheffield Steeldogs (15 saves), 30 Oct v MK Lightning (23), 21 Jan v Bracknell Bees (23), 5 Mar at Sheffield Steeldogs (24); play-offs: 22 March v Hull Pirates (14)*

English Premier League

Basingstoke Bison's top points scorers Ciaran Long (left) and Rene Jarolin (right).
(Photos by Lucy McGill Photography)

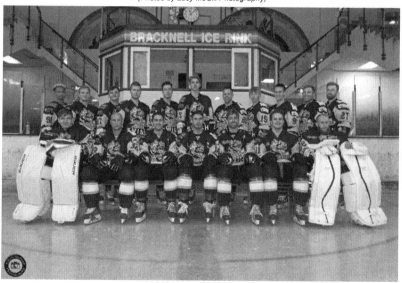

Bracknell Bees Team Photo by Kevin Slyfield
Back Row (left to right): Rio Grinell-Parke, Martin Pavlicek, Harvey Stead, David Gaborcik, Krystof Kafan, Joshua Tetlow, Carl Graham, Jack Hayes, Luka Basic, Carl Thompson, Josh Smith
Back Row: Matt Smital, Lukas Smital, James Galazzi, Matt Foord, Scott Spearing, Alex Barker, Alex Mettam

BRACKNELL BEES
Back to Basic

By DAVE WRIGHT *Bracknell News*

After some uncertainty in the 2016 close season, supporters **Carol Miller** and **Matt Fettel** joined forces with player-coach **Lukas Smital** to enable the Bees to survive in the English Premier League.

But again the team struggled on the ice.

A small budget and a depleted roster were largely to blame for the lack of success. Moreover, top scoring Brit **Ivan Antonov** had departed for rivals Basingstoke Bison in the summer, while **Shaun Thompson** only returned from Hampshire in mid-season to play with his brother Carl.

Slovenian winger **Luka Basic** and Slovakian defender **David Gaborcik** piled up the points but could do little to lift the club's fortunes.

It wasn't until 5 November that the Bees recorded their first home win, and even that was a close 3-2 affair with fellow strugglers Manchester Phoenix.

In January they signed **Rupert Quiney** from Guildford Flames, only for the 6ft 4in defenceman to damage his shoulder on his home debut and miss the rest of the season. He was joined on the sidelines by the influential **Scott Spearing**, who was unable to shake off a knee problem.

The team never looked capable of becoming serious challengers for the Play-offs and when the Phoenix dropped out, Bracknell were left adrift at the foot of the league table.

The mainly young squad conceded too many soft goals - even though netminder **Alex Mettam** frequently picked up the man-of-the-match award - while failing to take scoring chances at the other end. It was a steep learning curve for the youngsters.

• The Bees were deeply saddened when rink boss **John Nike**, who had supported the club so generously for many years, passed away at Christmas.

PLAYER AWARDS
Players' Player: **Carl Thompson**
Player of the Year: **David Gaborcik**
Best Forward: **Shaun Thompson**
Best Defenceman: **David Gaborcik**
Coach's Player: **Matt Foord**
Most Improved Player: **Rio Grinell-Parke**
Best British Player (Colin White Memorial Trophy):
Unsung Hero (Keith Robinson Memorial Trophy):
Scott Spearing

FACT FILE 2016-17
English Premier League: Ninth
Play-offs: Did not qualify
Premier Cup: Ninth in qualifying group

LEADING PLAYERS
Scott Spearing *born 26 April 1986, Swindon*
The hard driving, competitive forward was badly missed when he injured a knee but he stayed around assisting his teammates and the coaching staff on the bench.

Shaun Thompson *born 13 July 1987, Slough*
The tenacious forward gave the Bees extra firepower and experience, with his high workrate making him a firm fans' favourite.

MOST PROMISING PLAYER
Rio Grinell-Parke *born 25 February 1999, London*
The GB under-18 forward displayed increased confidence, and his good positional sense was rewarded with a few goals.

HISTORY: Founded: 1987 by John Nike Leisuresport. **Leagues**: English Premier League (EPL) 200516; British National League (BNL) 200305; Superleague 1996-2003; British League (BL), Premier Div. 1991-95; BL, Div. One 1995-96, 1990-91; English League 1987-90. **Honours**: See *The Ice Hockey Annual 2016-17*.

English Premier League

BRACKNELL BEES – PLAYER STATISTICS 2016/17

PLAYER Scorers	LEAGUE				
	GP	G	A	Pts	Pim
Luka Basic (I)	44	17	25	42	36
Alex Barker	47	18	21	39	22
David Gaborcik (I)	45	7	26	33	32
Shaun Thompson 1	27	14	17	31	24
Lukas Smital (I)	42	12	18	30	94
Carl Thompson	46	10	14	24	6
Olegs Lascenko (I)	41	8	9	17	4
Scott Spearing	36	5	12	17	68
Harvey Stead	46	2	13	15	55
James Galazzi	46	5	8	13	119
Martin Pavlicek (I)	45	3	9	12	4
Matt Foord	42	1	8	9	54
Josh Smith	34	3	4	7	20
Rio Grinell-Parke	43	3	1	4	14
Krystof Kafan (I)	18	2	2	4	20
Josh Tetlow	42	0	4	4	153
Danny Ingoldsby	35	2	1	3	45
Carl Graham	17	0	1	1	8
Jack Hayes	47	0	1	1	12
Winning shots		1		1 .	
Bench penalties					10
TEAM TOTALS	**48**	**113**	**194**	**307**	**800**

Netminders	GPI	Mins	SOG	GA	Sv%
Alex Mettam	44	2454	1455	190	86.9
Matt Smital	10	439	268	41	84.7
Winning shots				3	
Empty net goals			3	3	
TEAM TOTALS	**48**	**2893**	**1726**	**237**	**86.3**

Also appeared: *Rupert Quiney 2*
Also played for: *1 Basingstoke Bison; 2 Guildford Flames*

English Premier League

Guildford Flames
Winning Era Ends With A Whimper

By ANDY SMITH

After capturing 11 trophies in their 12 English Premier League seasons, the Flames ended the era with their worst league standing in 20 years and failed to emulate their Cup and Playoff double of the previous campaign.

Finnish netminder **Richard Ullberg** returned along with top scorers, Swede **Jens Erikson**, Slovene **Matic Krajl** and - for a fourth campaign - **Marcus Kristofferson**. Completing the import quota was Slovakian attacker **Marek Maslonka**.

But the season started weakly with the defence of the Cup in jeopardy after only a few games. Ullberg was released and **Dean Skinns** was brought out of retirement to share the goaling spot with the short-lived **Joonas Kuusela**.

Season-ending injuries to Kristoffersen and Krajl left Guildford languishing in the lower half of the table, but former Finnish Elite League veterans **Kari Shivonen** and **Tuomas Santavuori** helped to steady the ship over a more encouraging Christmas and New Year period.

The announcement that the club had applied to join the Elite League seemed to throw the team out of focus. With qualification for the Play-offs assured, too, little effort was shown for the rest of the league season and the Flames ended fifth.

A fourth netminder, Sussex native **Mike Will**, took over for the Play-off run and the Flames claimed a remarkable 11 of 12 points, duly gaining a place in the Coventry finals.

In an enthralling semi-final they were locked 3-3 with MK Lightning with 10 minutes left. Then the Lightning struck with five unanswered goals...

With the majority of the players knowing they would not be returning for the Elite League campaign, the Flames cut a sad image as they left the ice, especially the former Guildford juniors, **David Savage**, **Andy Hemmings** and **Tom Duggan**: though never big stars they always showed great commitment to the cause throughout the EPIHL era.

PLAYER AWARDS

Players' Player: **Ben Campbell**
Player of the Year: **Ben Campbell**
Top Points Scorer: **Ben Campbell**
Players' British Player: **Ben Campbell**
Fans' British Player: **Ben Campbell**
Sportsmanship Award: **Kevin Phillips**

FACT FILE 2016-17

English Premier League: Fifth
Play-offs: Semi-finalists
Premier Cup: Seventh in qualifying group

LEADING PLAYERS

Ben Campbell *born 16 May 1987, Durham*
Swept the board with five trophies at the club's awards night after finishing on top of the Flames' scoring charts. In his seven seasons, he made 399 appearances, scoring 140 goals and 329 points.

Andy Hemmings *born 15 August 1988, Guildford*
The home town favourite first iced for the Flames as a junior in 2002-03. A perfect utility forward, he is as much at home grinding on the fourth line as he is mixing with the stars on the first.

MOST PROMISING PLAYER

Jared Lane *born 31 March 1998, Chertsey, Surrey*
The captain of the club's under20 side iced 38 times for the Flames and an ovation greeted his first Spectrum goal.

HISTORY: Founded: 1992. **Leagues:** English Premier League 2005-17; British National League 1997-2005; (Southern) Premier League 1996-98; British League, Div. 1 1993-96; English League 1992/93.
Honours: *English Premier League*: Play-off Champions 2015-16, 201011; league winners 2012-13, 2011-12, 2007-08, 200506; Cup 201516, 201213, 2011-12, 2009-10, 200607.

English Premier League

Guildford Flames – Player Statistics 2016/17

PLAYER	LEAGUE					PLAY-OFFS				
Scorers	GP	G	A	Pts	Pim	GP	G	A	Pts	Pim
Ben Campbell	45	30	30	60	20	7	3	2	5	2
Jens Eriksson (I)	46	18	40	58	64	7	0	1	1	8
Marek Maslonka (I)	39	26	13	39	131	7	1	4	5	4
Danny Meyers	46	10	31	41	16	7	1	2	3	4
Tuomas Santavuori (I)	31	13	23	36	26	7	3	4	7	4
Jez Lundin	46	9	30	39	80	7	2	2	4	6
Michal Satek (I)	22	14	20	34	6	7	2	4	6	0
Tom Duggan	44	13	19	32	92	7	1	3	4	0
Matic Kralj (I)	22	11	24	35	39					
Andrew Mckinney	41	9	15	24	118	7	4	3	7	14
Kevin Phillips	46	6	11	17	46	7	0	0	0	0
Kari Sihvonen (I)	14	2	8	10	82	7	1	4	5	29
Andrew Hemmings	46	5	5	10	14	7	2	2	4	2
David Savage	29	4	7	11	4	7	1	2	3	0
Marcus Kristofferson (I)	11	2	6	8	58					
Sam Godfrey	25	0	4	4	28	7	0	2	2	2
Samuel Waller	40	0	3	3	20	7	0	1	1	0
Andrew Melachrino	21	1	1	2	35					
Jared Lane	36	1	1	2	4	2	0	0	0	0
Richard Ullberg (I) (N)	6	0	1	1	0					
Rupert Quiney 1	22	0	1	1	6					
Dean Skinns (N)	31	0	1	1	0	7	0	0	0	0
Jakub Kubis (I)	5	0	0	0	2					
Joonas Kuusela (I) (N)	13	0	0	0	2					
Winning shots		2		2			0		0	
Bench penalties					12					0
TEAM TOTALS	**48**	**176**	**294**	**470**	**905**	**7**	**21**	**36**	**57**	**75**

Netminders	LEAGUE					PLAY OFFS				
	GPI	Mins	SOG	GA	Sv%	GPI	Mins	SOG	GA	Sv%
Mike Will	12	619	296	30	89.9	7	439	186	16	91.4
Dean Skinns	24	1386	681	73	89.3					
Joonas Kuusela (I)	10	543	289	35	87.9					
Richard Ullberg (I)	6	340	188	28	85.1					
Winning shots				3					0	
Empty net goals			3	3				1	1	
TEAM TOTALS	**48**	**2888**	**1457**	**172**	**88.2**	**7**	**439**	**187**	**17**	**90.9**

Also played for: *1 Bracknell Bees.*

Shutouts:
Skinns (2) - league: 5 Nov at Basingstoke Bison (28 saves), 27 Dec v Bracknell Bees (22).
Will - play-offs: 22 March at Telford Tigers (24).

Guildford Flames Team Photo by John Uwins

Back Row L to R: Sam Smith (Equipment and 1st aid), Stuart Potts (Assistant Coach), David Savage, Andy McKinney, Sam Waller, Matic Kralj, Marcus Kristoffersson, Rupert Quiney, Danny Meyers, Jakub Kubis, Sam Godfrey, Ben Campbell, Marek Maslonka, Jens Eriksson, Jared Lane, Milos Melicherik (Assistant Coach), Paul Dixon (Head Coach & GM)
Front Row L to R: Mike Will, Tom Duggan, Jez Lundin, Joonas Kuusela, Kevin Phillips, Andy Melachrino, Andy Hemmings, Dean Skinns Missing: Michal Satek, Tuomas Santavuori, Kari Sihvonen

Hull Pirates Team Photo by Lois Tomlinson Photography.

Back Row (L-R): Nathan Craze (Assistant Coach), Scott Glenwright (Equipment Manager), Jonathon Kirk, Sam Towner, Jordan Fisher, Ugnius Cizas, Marcus Maynard, Martin Ondrej, Ryan Watt, Tommi Laine, Josh Gent, Jordan Stokes, Lee Bonner, Mike Forbes (Assistant Coach).
Front Row (L-R): Vlastimil Lakosil, Lee Haywood, Jamie Chilcott, Dominic Osman, Jason Hewitt (Head Coach), Nathan Salem, Luke Boothroyd, Andrej Themar, Ashley Smith.

See more great photos at http://hullhockey.wixsite.com/loisphotography

English Premier League

HULL PIRATES
A season of shameless clichés

By **CATHY WIGHAM** *Hull Daily Mail*

A GAME of two halves is a well-worn, tired cliché in sport. Well, Hull Pirates' 2016-17 English Premier League season will surely be remembered as "a campaign of two halves".

There were the halcyon days of September and October when the Pirates won 15 out of their first 20 games – including beating eventual champions Telford Tigers 6-0 and runners-up Milton Keynes 5-1.

Sure, the team shipped too many goals for comfort, but with **Andrej Themar**, **Nathan Salem** and **Stanislav Lascek** to spearhead the forwards, scoring wasn't a problem.

So far so good, but then team changes, intended to bridge the gap to the summit, back-fired badly. They seemed fine on paper: in late November coach **Dominic Osman** switched an attack-minded defenceman - **Jaroslav Sarsok** - for a more defensively solid blueliner - **Martin Ondrej** - to shore up a creaking defence.

In December **Tommi Laine**, Pirates' top scorer from 2015-16, returned to bolster the squad. The following month Osman ditched British-born netminder **Jordan Marr** and signed Czech **Vlastimil Lakosil**.

In late January, the league's leading assists man Lascek was axed for gross misconduct, and experienced forward **Jason Hewitt** picked up a season-ending shoulder injury, denting the team's ambitions still further.

To compound matters, forward **Ryan Watt** punched his way into a season-ending suspension, and Osman stepped down to concentrate on the club's business side, with Hewitt taking over as coach.

The Pirates couldn't buy a win and their 2016-17 ship sailed into a seventh place league finish and a first round play-off exit. "A season of two halves" and "a season of what ifs" will be forever etched into the record books.

PLAYER AWARDS
Most Valuable Player: **Andrej Themar**
Best Forward: **Ugnius Cizas**
Best Defenceman: **Jamie Chilcott**
Coach's Player: **Josh Gent**
Most Improved Player: **Jordan Stokes**
Unsung Hero: **Jon Kirk**

FACT FILE 2016-17
English Premier League: Seventh
Play-offs: Fourth in quarter-final group
Premier Cup: Semi-finalists

LEADING PLAYERS
Jon Kirk *born 21 August 1995, Maltby, S Yorks*
At 5ft 6in the blueliner was not the biggest on the team but a no frills, no fuss Yorkshireman who could mix it with the best.

Andrej Themar *born 28 June 1988, Slovakia*
New to Britain, the winger was an all-round talent, a great skater with a great shot. He was a big hit for the Pirates, top scoring by a massive 49 points with 50 goals and 43 assists.

MOST PROMISING PLAYER: Lee Bonner *born 7 April 1997, Hull*

A pocket rocket of a forward and a fans' favourite, due to his tenacity and never-say-die spirit. A GB junior international, he ended with 16 goals and 34 points, right behind the club's 'big three' scorers.

HISTORY: Founded: July 2015 by Shane Smith. Previous Hull teams were **Stingrays** 2003-15, **Thunder** 19992003, **Kingston Hawks** 199699, **Humberside (Sea)Hawks** 1988-96. **Leagues**: English Premier League 2015-17, 2005-06; Elite League 2006-15; British National League 200305. **Honours**: None. *Humberside Hawks* – see *The Ice Hockey Annual 2016-17*.

English Premier League

HULL PIRATES – PLAYER STATISTICS 2016/17

PLAYER	LEAGUE					PLAY-OFFS				
Scorers	GP	G	A	Pts	Pim	GP	G	A	Pts	Pim
Andrej Themar (I)	45	46	36	82	42	5	4	5	9	2
Nathan Salem	48	20	23	43	85	6	0	0	0	2
Stanislav Lascek (I) 1	28	13	30	43	56					
Lee Bonner	28	12	22	34	84					
Jason Hewitt	46	12	14	26	52	6	2	4	6	2
Ugnius Cizas (I)	39	13	14	27	12	6	2	2	4	2
Jonathan Kirk	48	6	17	23	18	6	1	2	3	0
James Chilcott	47	4	21	25	38	6	1	0	1	2
Dominic Osman (I)	34	12	12	24	22	6	0	1	1	2
Lee Haywood	48	3	19	22	42	6	1	1	2	8
Tommi Laine (I)	19	2	11	13	2	6	1	2	3	0
Ryan Watt	41	3	13	16	171					
Jaroslav Sarsok (I)	19	3	10	13	10					
Josh Gent	48	6	5	11	8	6	1	0	1	0
Marcus Maynard 3	43	0	8	8	74	6	0	0	0	12
Andrew Hirst 1	16	5	1	6	6	6	0	0	0	2
Sam Towner 2	14	0	4	4	4	6	1	1	2	0
Jordan Stokes	45	0	6	6	31	6	0	0	0	2
Jordan Fisher	39	2	2	4	22	6	0	1	1	4
Luke Boothroyd	12	0	2	2	10	6	0	2	2	8
Martin Ondrej (I)	19	0	3	3	63					
Gareth O'Flaherty 3	9	0	1	1	0					
Bradley Betteridge	12	0	0	0	2					
Vlastimil Lakosil (I) (N)	16	0	0	0	2	4	0	0	0	0
Jordan Marr (N)	31	0	0	0	2					
Ashley Smith (N)	42	0	0	0	2	2	0	0	0	0
Bench penalties					18					0
TEAM TOTALS	**48**	**162**	**274**	**436**	**878**	**6**	**14**	**21**	**35**	**48**

	LEAGUE					PLAY OFFS				
Netminders	GPI	Mins	SOG	GA	Sv%	GPI	Mins	SOG	GA	Sv%
Jordan Marr	28	1623	1010	88	91.3					
Vlastimil Lakosil (I)	16	934	655	71	89.2	4	240	159	21	86.8
Ashley Smith	8	322	198	38	80.8	2	125	71	12	83.1
Empty net goals			4	4				1	1	
TEAM TOTALS	**48**	**2879**	**1867**	**201**	**89.2**	**6**	**365**	**231**	**34**	**85.3**

Also appeared: *Aaron Burton, Bradley Moore (2), Cain Taylor, Joe Gent, Nathan Craze (N), Scott McKenzie.*
Also played for: *1 Sheffield Steeldogs; 2 Peterborough Phantoms; 3 Telford Tigers.*

Shutouts:
Marr- league: 1 Oct v Peterborough Phantoms (30 saves), 29 Oct v Telford Tigers (46).
Lakosil – league: 4 Feb v Bracknell Bees (28 saves).

English Premier League

MANCHESTER PHOENIX
From Blackpool to Widnes
By PAUL BREEZE

The announcement that the Phoenix would play their opening games of the 2016/17 EPL season at the Fylde Coast Ice Arena in Blackpool came as quite a shock to most people – especially those who knew the venue already and knew that its spectating facilties were rather "limited".

But this was only going to be for a few months while the new rink in Manchester was being completed, so long-suffering fans who had spent the previous season commuting back and forth to Deeside for home games could surely manage a few trips to sunny Blackpool to follow their team...?

Unfortunately, the club's tenure at FCIA lasted longer than initially anticipated as the completion date for the new permanent rink became vaguer and vaguer and the proposal for a temporary rink in Manchester also came and went without ever gaining any substance.

Now, running any ice hockey team is expensive and trying to run a competitive EPL team with imports and well-paid British players is hard to enough to manage at the best of times, so trying to do that at a rink that is some 60 miles away from your home fan-base and can only accommodate a few hundred paying supporters at best was always going to be a struggle. The team struggled on the ice as well as off it and only won 5 games in the period up to the end of the year.

It came as no great surprise, therefore, when in January 2017, Phoenix owner Neil Morris announced that the club had reached the end of the road financially and that drastic steps needed to be taken to try and keep it afloat until the end of the season.

All the paid players were axed - with most moving to other clubs - and the team opted to soldier on with young British players only, using guest players in a number of games to bolster the ranks.

Home games were switched to Widnes so as to offer a shorter journey for the Manchester-based fans to go and watch their team play and this paid off as crowds jumped to around the 350 mark but, needless to say, the team was now hopelessly outclassed and only managed to muster 5 goals in their last 5 league games.

There were rumours of a new consortium coming in to take over the club and keep it going to the end of season – with the team based at Widnes – and hopes that a long term solution might still be found. Unfortunately, the end of January arrived with nothing being put in place and the club had to withdraw from the league.

The last Manchester Phoenix game took place on 29th January at Silver Blades Widnes against Swindon Wildcats. The result was a 3-11 victory for the visitors and the last Phoenix goal was scored at 50.32 by Miles Dacres – usually of Bradford Bulldogs in the NIHL Laidler Conference - who was making a guest appearance and scored two goals in his only ever EPL game.

The rink that never was. An artist's impression of the Phoenix's new Manchester rink that was never built.

English Premier League

MANCHESTER PHOENIX – PLAYER STATISTICS 2016/17

League Matches Up to 29th January 2017

Player	GP	G	A	Pts	PIM	List Of Matches Played 2016/17
Robin Kovar	34	19	26	45	39	10th Sep: Hull Pirates – H Lost 4 - 11
Edgars Bebris	32	18	26	44	28	11th Sep: Telford Tigers – A Lost 1 - 4
Roman Malinik	28	17	13	30	8	17th Sep: Swindon Wildcats – A Lost 2 - 5
Joni Tuominen	31	4	17	21	46	18th Sep: M/Keynes Lightning – H Lost 1 - 3
James Neil	38	3	16	19	0	24th Sep: Bracknell Bees – H Lost 2 - 7
Marek Indra	20	5	10	15	20	25th Sep: Bracknell Bees – A Won 5 - 0
Vaclav Meidl	18	6	8	14	26	1st Oct: Telford Tigers – A Lost 2 - 4
Gareth O'Flaherty	28	5	6	11	8	2nd Oct: Swindon Wildcats – H Lost 1 - 5
Luke Boothroyd	38	0	9	9	54	8th Oct: Sheffield Steeldogs – A Lost 1 - 4
Jakub Langhammer	16	4	5	9	8	9th Oct: Guildford Flames – H Lost 2 - 4
Ben Wood	33	4	3	7	10	15th Oct: Guildford Flames – A Won 4 - 3 (P)
Scott William Bailey	35	1	5	6	6	16th Oct: Basingstoke Bison – A Lost 2 - 7
Craig Thurston	9	2	3	5	0	22nd Oct: M/Keynes Lightning – A Lost 2 - 6
Lewis James Baldwin	37	1	3	4	8	23rd Oct: Bracknell Bees - H Won 8 - 5
Greg Pick	38	0	4	4	22	26th Oct: Hull Pirates – A Lost 2 - 6
Michael John Stratford	19	2	2	4	6	30th Oct: Hull Pirates –H Lost 3 - 4 (Pens)
Myles David Dacres	1	2	0	2	0	5th Nov: Bracknell Bees – A Lost 2 - 3
Lloyd Gibson	1	1	0	1	0	6th Nov: Peterboro' Phantoms – H Lost 1 - 6
Ross Michael Kennedy	1	0	1	1	0	12th Nov: Basingstoke Bison – A Lost 2 - 5
Ryan Mcfarlane	3	0	1	1	2	13th Nov: M/Keynes Lightning – H Lost 3 - 12
Grant Richardson	3	0	1	1	0	19th Nov: Swindon Wildcats – A Lost 2 - 3
James Hepburn Riddoch	1	0	1	1	0	20th Nov: Sheffield Steeldogs – H Won 5 - 2
Robert Streetly	2	0	1	1	2	26th Nov: Telford Tigers – H Lost 2 - 5
Michael Peter Whillock	1	1	0	1	0	27th Nov: Peterboro' Phantoms – A Lost 1 - 9
Geoff Wigglesworth	1	0	1	1	0	3rd Dec: Guildford Flames – A Lost 3 - 5
Thomas Asprey	3	0	0	0	4	4th Dec: B'stoke Bison – H Won 2 - 1 (OT)
Denis Bell	32	0	0	0	0	11th Dec: Sheffield Steeldogs – H Won 4 - 2
Daniel Bullock	1	0	0	0	0	17th Dec: Sheffield Steeldogs – A Lost 2 - 8
Alexander Cole	1	0	0	0	0	27th Dec: Telford Tigers – H Lost 1 - 10
Darren Elliott	1	0	0	0	0	2nd Jan: Hull Pirates – H Lost 3 - 6
Stephen Fone	38	0	0	0	0	7th Jan: Guildford Flames – H Lost 1 - 7
Ryan Johnson	1	0	0	0	0	8th Jan: Hull Pirates – A Lost 5 - 11
Matthew Lawday	1	0	0	0	0	14th Jan: Guildford Flames – A Lost 5 - 11
Adam Mcnicoll	1	0	0	0	0	15th Jan: Peterboro' Phantoms – H Lost 0 - 7
Ross Miller	1	0	0	0	0	21st Jan: Swindon Wildcats – A Lost 0 - 5
Scott Morris	1	0	0	0	2	27th Jan: Sheffield Steeldogs – A Lost 1-7
Philip Mulcahy	1	0	0	0	0	28th Jan: Bracknell Bees – A Lost 1-5
Ben Paynter	1	0	0	0	0	29th Jan: Swindon Wildcats – H Lost 3-11
Giacomo Raffaelli	1	0	0	0	0	
James Spurr	1	0	0	0	0	
Alexander Trendall	1	0	0	0	0	
Mark Turner	1	0	0	0	0	
Craig Wallis	1	0	0	0	0	
Mason Wild	1	0	0	0	0	*Home games up to and including 7th*
Bailey Martin Wootton	1	0	0	0	0	*January 2017 played at Fylde Coast Ice*
Taylor Martin Wootton	1	0	0	0	0	*Arena, Blackpool*
Callum Worthington-Evans	1	0	0	0	0	*Home games on 15th and 29th January*
Team Totals		**95**	**162**	**257**	**299**	*played at Silver Blades Rink, Widnes*

Netminder	GPI	Minutes	Saves	Goals	Save%
Denis Bell	12	274:40	201	33	83.6%
Empty Net	6	02:20	0	0	
Winning Shoot-Out Goals				1	
Ross Miller	1	02:09	2	0	
Stephen Fone	37	2011:23	1541	186	
Team Totals		**2290:32**	**1744**	**220**	

24

English Premier League

Manchester Phoenix Team Photo by Hollie Godber

L-R: Myles Dacres, James Neil, Steve Fone, Luke Boothroyd, Vaclav Miedl, Gareth O'Flaherty, Craig Thurston, Robin Kovar, Greg Pick, Scott Bailey, Lewis Baldwin, Joni Tuominen, Denis Bell. Ben Wood & Craig Cooke (kit mg)

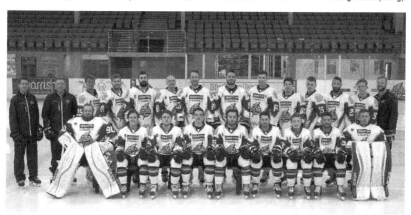

Milton Keynes Lightning Team Photo by Tony Sargent

Back row (left to right): Grant McPherson (assistant coach), Peter Russell (head coach), Antti Hölli, Lewis Hook, Mikolaj Lopuski, Blaz Emersic, Tom Carlon, Frantisek Bakrlik, Leigh Jamieson, Craig Scott, James Griffin, Milan Baranyk, Ed Knaggs, Lewis Clifford (assistant coach).
Front row: Przemyslaw Odrobny, Luc Johnson, Jordan Cownie, Michael Farn, Adam Carr (captain), Lewis Christie, Glenn Billing, James Neil, Jordan Hedley

MILTON KEYNES LIGHNING
Ended with a double
PAUL BROOKMAN

Milton Keynes Lightning ended their 15-year spell in the English Premier League triumphantly, collecting the Play-off and Cup double.

The club had announced at the end of season 2015-16 that they intended to move up to the Elite League so coach **Pete Russell** made his key 2016-17 signings with this in mind.

They included two Polish internationals, netminder **Przemyslaw Odrobny** and forward **Mikolaj Lopuski**, who inked two-year deals, and former Czech under-20 forward **Milan Baranyk**, 36, from Peterborough Phantoms.

Also signed from the Phantoms was British-Canadian winger **Craig Scott**, the son of **Patrick (Paddy) Scott**, who was a legend with the town's team in the 1990s.

Odrobny turned out to be the best goalie ever to wear the Lightning's shirt, earning the nickname the Great Wall of Milton Keynes, due to his 6ft 4in stature and reliability.

Lopuski's season, however, was interrupted by injury after just seven games, and the team brought in Finn **Antti Hölli**. When the Pole returned in February, the team rotated six imports until Baranyk was side-lined for the final games.

In the league the Lightning trailed for much of the season in second place behind the controversial eventual champions Telford Tigers, but they were more successful in the Cup, beating their great rivals, the Phantoms.

But that was eclipsed just a couple of weeks later in the Play-off final at Coventry. They took a 5-0 lead into the second break and went on to demolish the Tigers 7-2, winning the Playoffs for the first time since 2006.

Russell said: "We were on a different level. We came together as one and we were on fire. It was absolutely amazing. The memories will stick with us forever."

PLAYER AWARDS

Players' Player : **'Przemy' Odrobny**
Most Valuable Play: **'Przemy' Odrobny**
Top Scorer: **Lewis Hook**
Best Defenceman: **Lewis Christie**
Coach's Award: **Blaz Emersic**
Most Improved Player: **Luc Johnson**

FACT FILE 2016-17

English Premier League: Runners-up
Play-offs: Champions
Premier Cup: Winners

MOST PROMISING PLAYER

Glenn Billing *born 28 May 1997, Romford*
After missing early games through injury, his confidence grew and, with his fellow GB under20 international **Luc Johnson**, provided a spark in difficult moments.

LEADING PLAYERS

Blaz Emersic *born 10 October 1980, Slovenia*
Reliable and experienced forward never sought the limelight but was always ready to score vital goals when needed.

Przemyslaw Odrobny *born 21 October 1985, Gdansk, Poland*
The popular Polish international keeper - the fans shortened his first name to 'Przemy', pronounced 'Shemmy' - was a key to his team's success with three league shutouts.

HISTORY. Founded: 2002 by **Harry Howton** and **Nick Poole**. Run by rink operators Planet Ice 2013-17. (The original club in Milton Keynes was formed in 1990 as *Kings*. For more see *The Ice Hockey Annual 2015-16.*) **Leagues:** English Premier League (EPIHL) 2002-17.
Honours: EPIHL 2009-10, 200305; EPIHL Play-offs 2016-17, 2002-06; EPIHL Cup 2016-17.

English Premier League

MILTON KEYNES LIGHTNING - PLAYER STATISTICS 2016/17

PLAYER	LEAGUE					PLAY-OFFS				
Scorers	GP	G	A	Pts	Pim	GP	G	A	Pts	Pim
Lewis Hook	48	26	22	48	14	8	6	8	14	4
Frantisek Bakrlik (I)	44	24	21	45	162	5	5	4	9	29
Antti Holli (I)	28	10	27	37	16	8	7	8	15	2
Jordan Cownie	39	11	30	41	41	8	3	7	10	4
Craig Scott	48	13	20	33	6	8	4	11	15	0
Milan Baranyk (I)	43	17	28	45	45	3	0	2	2	0
Blaz Emersic (I)	47	11	21	32	14	8	7	3	10	2
Adam Carr	46	12	16	28	10	8	0	3	3	2
Michael Farn	42	3	20	23	45	6	0	5	5	0
James Griffin	47	10	14	24	102	6	2	0	2	8
Leigh Jamieson	47	2	20	22	50	8	2	1	3	10
Tom Carlon	40	9	13	22	71	8	2	2	4	6
Mikolaj Lopuski (I)	16	5	8	13	24	8	4	4	8	2
Bobby Chamberlain	24	11	9	20	104					
Lewis Christie	47	2	9	11	57	8	0	4	4	0
Sam Jones	32	4	8	12	57					
James Neil	13	0	7	7	0	8	0	3	3	0
Glenn Billing	41	2	4	6	4	8	0	1	1	0
Luc Johnson	45	0	3	3	16	8	1	1	2	0
Edward Knaggs	43	0	4	4	6	8	0	1	1	0
Przemyslaw Odrobny (I) (N)	47	0	4	4	8	7	0	0	0	2
Winning shots		2		2			0		0	
Bench penalties					4					2
TEAM TOTALS	**48**	**174**	**308**	**482**	**856**	**8**	**43**	**68**	**111**	**73**

	LEAGUE					PLAY OFFS				
Netminders	GPI	Mins	SOG	GA	Sv%	GPI	Mins	SOG	GA	Sv%
Pzremyslaw Odrobny (I)	47	2757	1559	111	92.9	7	420	224	18	92.0
Jordan Hedley	7	137	74	11	85.1	1	59	20	1	95.0
Chris Jenkins						1	1	2	1	50.0
Winning shots			0					0		
Empty net goals			2	2				0	0	
TEAM TOTALS	**48**	**2894**	**1635**	**124**	**92.4**	**8**	**480**	**246**	**20**	**92.2**

Also appeared: *Grant McPherson.*

Shutouts: *Odrobny (3) - league: 2 Dec v Basingstoke Bison (46 saves), 11 Dec at Hull Pirates (30), 27 Dec at Peterborough Phantoms (43).*

English Premier League

PETERBOROUGH PHANTOMS
Young Team Just Miss Silverware

By PHIL SMITH

The Phantoms just missed out on third place in the English Premier League, and fought their way to the Cup final, only to lose to old rivals, Milton Keynes Lightning.

It was the Lightning in the summer of 2016 that had snapped up the Phantoms' top two scorers - **Craig Scott** and **Milan Baranyk** - giving rise to concern among the fans.

But coach **Slava Koulikov** retained most of his squad, including the high scoring **Darius Pliskauskas** and **Ales Padelek**, and persuaded experienced former Phantom, **James Archer**, to return to the fold.

Overall, the roster had a youthful complexion, with a number of talented prospects, and what the team lacked in games won, it made up for in effort.

Planet Ice Peterborough was a fortress before Christmas as Koulikov steered his men to wins over Guildford Flames (a shock 5-0 shutout), Telford Tigers (43 after a shootout) and Basingstoke Bison (21) and dropped just three points. In fact, they finished the season with only four league defeats on their own ice.

The highlight of the season was their qualification for the Cup final for the second year running, beating league champs Telford in the process.

After each side won its respective semifinal, newcomer **Wehebe Darge** converted the winner in the tie-break shootout. Goalie **Janis Auzins** - back for a third season - kept the Tigers at bay to secure his team's place in the final against the Lightning.

The Phantoms shaded their home leg 2-1, with Darge once more the game winner, but **Pete Russell**'s men took the second leg in Milton Keynes 3-0. **Adam Carr** broke the Phantoms' hearts when he converted the Lightning's fifth penalty shot to win the Cup.

PLAYER AWARDS
Players' Player: **Darius Pliskauskas**
Player of the Year: **Janis Auzins**
Coach's Player: **Robert Ferrara**
Best Forward: **Wehebe Darge**
Best Defenceman: **Tom Norton**
Most Improved Player: **Owen Griffiths**
Young Player of the Year: **Owen Griffiths**

FACT FILE 2016-17
English Premier League: Fourth
Play-offs: Third in quarter-final group
Premier Cup: Finalists

LEADING PLAYERS
Janis Auzins *born 8 May 1991, Riga, Latvia*
The super-stopper racked up more shutouts (seven) than any other keeper in the top leagues, and took his team to the Cup final with some acrobatic saves in the semi-final shootout.
Wehebe Darge *born 4 December 1991, Adelaide, Australia.*
The Aussie international playmaker showed energy, tenacity and will-to-win, which made him a cult hero among the fans.

MOST PROMISING PLAYER
Owen Griffiths *born 15 July 1996, Cardiff.*
The GB junior centreman from Swindon enjoyed a break-out season, finishing as one of the team's key players.

HISTORY
Founded: 2002 by **Phil Wing** and **Rob Housden**. In April 2015 the club was taken over by **Dave** and **Jo Lane**, directors of team sponsor *Dalrod*. (The previous team in Peterborough was the *Pirates* 19822002.)
League: English Premier League 200217.
Honours: League winners 2008-09, 2002-03; Play-offs 2014-15, 200809; Premier Cup 200809, 200304, 2002-03. *Pirates* - see *The Ice Hockey Annual 2010-11*.

English Premier League

PETERBOROUGH PHANTOMS – PLAYER STATISTICS 2016/17

PLAYER	LEAGUE					PLAY-OFFS				
	GP	G	A	Pts	Pim	GP	G	A	Pts	Pim
Darius Pliskauskas (I)	45	28	28	56	8	6	6	1	7	2
Ales Padelek (I)	46	31	24	55	18	6	1	5	6	0
Petr Stepanek (I)	45	19	33	52	65	6	6	2	8	2
Marc Levers	31	11	28	39	8	6	1	8	9	2
Wehebe Darge (I)	39	12	25	37	53	6	3	2	5	0
Tom Norton	46	6	26	32	38	6	1	4	5	0
James Archer	45	9	19	28	57	6	0	5	5	6
Martins Susters (I)	39	18	15	33	28					
Owen Griffiths	47	12	15	27	18	6	0	3	3	2
Edgars Bebris (I)	14	6	14	20	14	6	3	3	6	4
James Ferrara	44	10	15	25	36	6	1	1	2	0
Sam Towner 1	28	7	8	15	18					
Will Weldon	37	1	12	13	64	6	1	1	2	16
Scott Robson	37	1	10	11	20	6	2	1	3	6
Robert Ferrara	46	4	3	7	30	6	1	0	1	0
James White	46	2	5	7	10	6	0	0	0	0
Ben Russell	34	2	4	6	2	6	0	0	0	0
Tom Stubley	40	2	2	4	18	6	0	0	0	2
Janis Auzins (I) (N)	37	0	5	5	20	6	0	0	0	4
Greg Pick	10	1	2	3	20	6	0	0	0	2
Nathan Pollard	1	0	2	2	0					
Nathan Long	14	0	2	2	6					
Craig Wallis	24	0	2	2	6					
Conor Pollard	1	1	0	1	0					
Bradley Moore 1	16	1	0	1	0	6	0	0	0	0
Connor Glossop	17	0	1	1	2					
Callum Medcalf	15	0	1	1	2	1	0	0	0	0
Winning shots		2		2			0		0	
Bench penalties					14					0
TEAM TOTALS	48	186	301	487	575	6	26	36	62	48

		LEAGUE					PLAY OFFS			
Netminders	GPI	Mins	SOG	GA	Sv%	GPI	Mins	SOG	GA	Sv%
Dan Lane	1	8	4	0	100					
Janis Auzins (I)	37	2040	1125	82	92.7	6	320	164	17	90
Adam Long	24	830	495	55	88.9	2	36	15	2	86.7
Winning shots			2	2				0	0	
Empty net goals				2					0	
TEAM TOTALS	48	2878	1626	141	91.3	6	356	179	19	89.4

Also appeared: *Connor Stokes, Jack Peacock.*
Also played for: *1 Hull Pirates.*

Shutouts:
Auzins (6) - league: 29 Oct v Guildford Flames (33 saves), 20 Nov v Hull Pirates (30), 11 Dec v Bracknell Bees (37), 29 Dec at Bracknell Bees (38), *14 Jan at Swindon (36); play-offs: *22 March v Sheffield Steeldogs (30).

Long (2) - *14 Jan at Swindon Wildcats (1); playoffs: *22 March v Sheffield Steeldogs (1).
* shared

English Premier League

Peteborough Phantoms Team Photo by Tom Scott (AMO Photos)
Back row L-R: Rob Horspool (Equipment Manager), Connor Stokes, Nathan Long, Calllum Medcalf, Wehebe Darge, Ben Russell, James White, Ales Padelek, Petr Stepanek, Edgars Bebris, Scott Robson, Tom Stubley, Greg Pick, Darius Pliskauskas, Brad Moore
Front Row L-R: Janis Auzins, James Archer, Robert Ferrara, Tom Norton, Slava Koulikov (Head Coach), James Ferrara, Jason Buckman (Assistant Coach), Marc Levers, Will Weldon, Dan Lane, Adam Long   Not pictured: Owen Griffiths

Sheffield Steeldogs Team Photo by Peter Best Photography
Back Row: Andy Hirst, Tom Barry, Tim Smith, Tom Brcko, Callum Pattison, Pavel Mrna, Tom Relf, Cole Shudra, Cameron Brownley, Joe Colton, Angus Laing.
Font Row: James Hadfield, Donatas Kumeliauskas, Arnoldas Bosas, Ben Morgan, Greg Wood, Lewis Bell, Liam Charnock, Adrian Palak, Brandon Stones.

English Premier League

SHEFFIELD STEELDOGS
Five imports but few wins
By ROGER WILLIAMS

The 2016-17 (and last) English Premier League season started optimistically for the Steeldogs.

In his second year as player-coach, **Greg Wood** retained the services of league MVP **Arnoldas Bosas** and brought in his national teammate **Donatas Kumeliauskas**.

With five import slots to fill, Wood then added Czech forward **Pavel Mrna** and the Slovak pair of **Tomas Brcko** on defence and former Deeside Dragon **Adrian Palak** up front.

Some of the old guard moved on - **Lee Haywood** went to Hull and **Steve Duncombe** to Blackburn, while **Tom Relf** joined from Bracknell. Former Sheffield junior goalie **James Hadfield** returned after a year away from hockey as the club shunned the trend for import netminders.

Kumeliuaskas and Palak picked up significant injuries in the very first game of the season, setting the tone for a campaign where playing with a full complement of imports was the exception rather than the rule.

In their first game with a full strength bench in November, the Dogs crashed 3-0 at home to Bracknell. This triggered a wretched period when they managed only three wins in 23 games, including double-figure defeats by Basingstoke and Peterborough.

Macaulay Heywood joined from Telford and **Andrew Hirst** headed off to the Pirates but it needed a more significant change to turn things around.

After releasing penalty box resident **Pavel Mrna** at the end of December, Wood turned to **Stanislav (Stano) Lascek**, one of their top scorers in 2015-16, who had moved to Hull.

He brought balance to the team and helped to keep them out of last place - but a pointless Play-off campaign ended the season on a down note.

PLAYER AWARDS
Players' Player: **Tomas Brcko**
Player of the Year: **Ashley Calvert**
Most Valuable Player: **Stanislav Lascek**
Coach's Player: **Arnoldas Bosas**
Best British Player: **Liam Kirk**
Unsung Hero: **Tomas Brcko**

FACT FILE 2016-17
English Premier League: Eighth
Play-offs: Fourth in quarter-final group
Premier Cup: Eighth in qualifying round

LEADING PLAYERS
Arnoldas Bosas *born 28 August 1990, Kaunas, Lithuania*
The team's star scorer, out-pointing his teammates by over 40 and ending as runnerup in league scoring. All this despite numerous changes to his line-mates.

Tomas Brcko *born 8 February 1988, Martin, Slovakia*
The defenceman's determined and committed play was a major asset to a struggling team.

MOST PROMISING PLAYER
Liam Kirk *born 1 March 2000, Rotherham, Yorks*
The first year senior wowed everyone as he was runner-up in the team's points and broke the EPIHL's scoring record for an under21 player, despite playing almost half the season with the Elite's Steelers.

HISTORY
Founded: 1994, playing out of the Queens Road, Sheffield rink. Transferred to iceSheffield in 2003. **Ali Cree** and **Robin Grayson** took control in November 2015.
Leagues: English Premier League 2005-17; English National League 2002-05; English Conference 200003, 1994-98; English League Div One 19982000.
Honours: None in English Premier League.

English Premier League

SHEFFIELD STEELDOGS – PLAYER STATISTICS 2016/17

PLAYER	LEAGUE					PLAY-OFFS				
	GP	G	A	Pts	Pim	GP	G	A	Pts	Pim
Arnoldas Bosas (I)	47	34	44	78	67	6	3	1	4	2
Liam Kirk	34	15	25	40	10					
Donatas Kumeliauskas (I)	33	13	17	30	47	5	1	1	2	2
Pavel Mrna (I)	20	19	10	29	170					
Macaulay Heywood 2	25	12	13	25	65	6	1	2	3	2
Ben Morgan	41	1	25	26	20	6	0	1	1	2
Stanislav Lascek (I) 1	12	10	9	19	16	6	2	4	6	0
Greg Wood	30	7	15	22	74	3	0	0	0	0
Cole Shudra	23	5	11	16	18	6	0	4	4	4
Adrian Palak (I)	35	6	13	19	30	3	0	0	0	8
Tomas Brcko (I)	47	5	13	18	18	6	0	0	0	0
Ashley Calvert	47	4	12	16	40	4	0	1	1	0
Tim Smith	46	3	13	16	26	5	0	0	0	35
Andrew Hirst 1	24	8	6	14	4					
Liam Charnock	40	4	9	13	30	6	0	0	0	4
Thomas Relf	42	1	8	9	16	6	0	0	0	2
Lewis Bell	47	0	8	8	48	6	1	0	1	6
Cameron Brownley	25	1	2	3	31	6	0	0	0	2
James Hadfield (N)	45	0	3	3	25	6	0	0	0	0
Jan Krivohlavek (I)	2	1	1	2	0					
Thomas Barry	46	1	1	2	24	6	0	0	0	14
Callum Pattison	25	1	0	1	197					
Lewis Baldwin	5	0	0	0	4					
Charles Thompson	31	0	0	0	48	6	0	0	0	0
Winning shots		2		2			0		0	
TEAM TOTALS	**48**	**153**	**258**	**411**	**1066**	**6**	**8**	**14**	**22**	**85**

	LEAGUE					PLAY OFFS				
Netminders	GPI	Mins	SOG	GA	Sv%	GPI	Mins	SOG	GA	Sv%
James Hadfield	43	2514	1656	184	88.9	5	278	162	26	84.0
Brandon Stones	9	370	282	34	87.9	2	80	53	13	75.5
Winning shots				3					0	
Empty net goals			4	4				0	0	
TEAM TOTALS	**48**	**2884**	**1942**	**225**	**88.4**	**6**	**358**	**215**	**39**	**81.9**

Also appeared: *Aaron Jepson, Angus Laing, George Crawshaw, Jamie Scott, Joe Cross, Joe Colton, Lloyd Gibson, Ryan Fraley, Tom Barkworth.*

Also played for: *1 Hull Pirates; 2 Telford Tigers.*

Shutouts:
Stones (2) - league: *6 Nov at Guildford Flames (7 saves), 7 Jan v Bracknell Bees (47).
Hadfield - league: *6 Nov at Guildford Flames (35 saves).   * shared.

English Premier League

SWINDON WILDCATS
Young Team, Old Story
By HARRY ABBOTT

WILDCATS

Swindon freshened their import line-up ahead of their English Premier League season. The newcomers were **Max Birbraer** (Telford Tigers) and **Mark Smith** (Cardiff Devils), as top scorers **Tomasz Malasinski** and **Jonas Hoog** were retained, along with captain **Jan Kostal**.

GB junior international **Ben Smith** was added for a brief early season stint ahead of his move to the USA, and a string of young players were promoted to the first team.

The 'Cats boasted a 5-5 W-L record from their opening ten fixtures but, as autumn turned to winter, a spate of injuries severely hampered them, including coach **Aaron Nell** and d-man **Callum Buglass**, who suffered season-ending knocks.

A run of eight defeats in ten games - including five in a row - followed, all but ending their hopes of regular season glory.

Swindon were now forced to rely on a raft of younger players, with **Ollie Stone**, **Kyle Smith**, **Ben Nethersell** and **Adam Finlinson** all stepping up admirably.

Former GB international **Phil Hill** signed in mid-season to add some experience, and even former Wildcats' coach **Ryan Aldridge** came out of retirement for six games. Injuries struck again in the New Year, though, with import defender Smith having his season curtailed, and **Robin Kovar** brought in to fill the void.

With a host of problems to contend with, the 'Cats finished in the bottom half of the table with 22 victories and 26 defeats.

Nell's side were always going to be up against it when they were placed in the same Play-off qualifying pool as league runners-up MK Lightning and third placed Basingstoke.

And so it proved as they won just twice, both times against fellow strugglers, Hull Pirates, the third season in a row they had missed the finals weekend in Coventry.

PLAYER AWARDS
Players' Player: **Jan Kostal**
Player of the Year: **Tomasz Malasinski**
Coach's Player: **Neil Liddiard**
Best Forward: **Tomasz Malasinski**
Best Defenceman: **Stevie Whitfield**
Best British Player (Dave Richardson Award): **Stevie Whitfield**
Most Improved Player: **Floyd Taylor**

FACT FILE 2016-17
English Premier League: Sixth
Play-offs: Third in quarter-final group
Premier Cup: Sixth in qualifying round

LEADING PLAYERS
Jan Kostal *born 13 April 1980, Karlovy Vary, Czech Republic.*
Leader, warrior and captain, the forward is the ultimate professional and a penalty killing machine.

Steve Whitfield *born 12 October 1990, Swindon*
The local prospect turned home town hero is a workhorse who battles for every puck on every shift and is a vital part of the team's defence.

MOST PROMISING PLAYER
Jordan Kelsall *born 12 August 1999, Nottingham*
A smooth skater with an accurate shot, the GB junior forward enjoyed a breakout season at EPIHL level while also icing for Okanagan Hockey Academy UK.

HISTORY
Founded: 2001 as Lynx. Reverted to original name of Wildcats in 2004. (Previous clubs in the Link Centre were *Phoenix* 2000-01, *Chill* 19972000, *IceLords* 1996-97 and *Wildcats* 1986-96.)
Leagues: *Wildcats* - English Premier League 200417 and British League, Div One 1986-96.
Honours: *Wildcats* - Autumn Trophy 1991-92.

English Premier League

SWINDON WILDCATS – PLAYER STATISTICS 2016/17

PLAYER	ENGLISH PREMIER					PLAY-OFFS				
	GP	G	A	Pts	Pim	GP	G	A	Pts	Pim
Tomasz Malasinski (I)	46	36	39	75	44	6	5	2	7	12
Jonas Hoog (I)	48	17	56	73	20	6	1	7	8	2
Maxim Birbraer (I)	45	14	26	40	126	6	6	3	9	2
Phil Hill 1	26	6	16	22	14	5	0	4	4	2
Aaron Nell	14	14	11	25	16					
Robin Kovar (I)	14	12	7	19	8	5	1	2	3	2
Neil Liddiard	48	2	15	17	104	6	1	4	5	4
Jan Kostal (I)	48	12	9	21	34	6	0	0	0	4
Stephen Whitfield	48	3	12	15	92	6	2	1	3	8
Lee Richardson	46	3	12	15	24	6	0	3	3	2
Ben Nethersell	35	3	10	13	4	6	0	2	2	2
Sam Bullas	36	6	4	10	62	5	2	2	4	12
Jordan Kelsall	30	8	4	12	16	3	1	0	1	0
Floyd Taylor	42	1	8	9	36	6	1	0	1	4
Mark Smith	31	2	7	9	26					
Ben Davies	5	5	3	8	4					
Toms Rutkis	23	4	2	6	27	6	0	2	2	0
Adam Finlinson	46	1	4	5	8	6	1	0	1	2
Kyle Smith	32	2	0	2	91	5	0	0	0	4
Michael Stratford	29	1	1	2	0	6	0	0	0	0
Ryan Aldridge	5	0	2	2	6					
Oliver Stone	35	0	1	1	16	6	0	1	1	0
Matt Selby	7	0	0	0	4					
Callum Buglass	12	0	0	0	4					
Stevie Lyle (N)	48	0	0	0	14	6	0	0	0	2
Winning shots		4		4			0		0	
Bench penalties					16					4
TEAM TOTALS	**48**	**156**	**249**	**405**	**816**	**6**	**21**	**33**	**54**	**68**

	LEAGUE					PLAY OFFS				
Netminders	GPI	Mins	SOG	GA	Sv%	GPI	Mins	SOG	GA	Sv%
Stevie Lyle	48	2867	1681	160	90.5	5	295	170	22	87.1
Michael Crisp	4	34	20	3	85.0	2	66	36	6	83.3
Winning shots				2					0	
Empty net goals			5	5				1	1	
TEAM TOTALS	**48**	**2901**	**1706**	**170**	**90.0**	**6**	**361**	**207**	**29**	**86.0**

Also appeared: *Deakan Fielder.*
Also played for: *1 Telford Tigers.*

Shutouts:
*Lyle - league: *4 Mar v Bracknell Bees
(21),
Crisp - league: *4 Mar v Bracknell Bees
(21).
* shared*

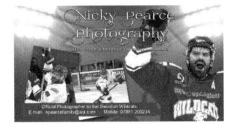

English Premier League

Swindon Wildcats Team Photo by Nicky Pearce Photography
Back Row (l to r): Oliver Stone, Adam Finlinson , Ben Nethersall, Sam Smith, Michael Stratford, Callum Buglass, Sam Bullas Toms Rutkis, Steve Whitfield, Ben Davis, Floyd Taylor, Kyle Smith. Front Row: Stevie Lyle, Max Birbraer Neil Liddiard, Aaron Nell, Jan Kostall, Lee Richardson, Jonus Hoog, Michael Crisp

Telford Tigers celebrate winning the English Premier League title (Photo by Steve Brodie / Tigers Photos)

English Premier League

TELFORD TIGERS
Bizarre
By ROB STUART

The Tigers' 2016-17 season in the English Premier League was as bizarre as any in the colourful 32-year history of hockey in Telford.

Tom Watkins, their long-suffering coach, somehow steered them through a major financial crisis to not only finish on top of the league, but also keep them at #1 for most of the year.

What's more, their final points total was 12 better than league runnersup, MK Lightning, and 22 more than the third placed Basingstoke Bison.

The money mess left players unpaid until November when the club was 'restructured' with new owners. But not before Czech goalie **Ondrej Raszka** had left for a better pay day in Poland, of all places.

He was replaced by talented young Brit, **Sam Gospel**, at least until ex-Bison **Jon Baston** made the Tigers his third EPIHL stop.

But it was the team's firepower and skill up front that carried them to the heights. The experienced Canadians **Doug Clarkson** and **Jason Silverthorn** bagged the goals while Hullborn playmaker **Matt Davies** tallied the most assists in the league.

Though the cash flow problem – aka winding up the ownership company and leaving debts - didn't affect the Tigers' play, it upset many of their league rivals, with some of them wanting to bar Telford from the play-offs.

This didn't happen, of course, but it meant that, through no fault of their own, Watkins and his men received a frosty reception from the other teams' fans in Coventry.

A last period powerplay goal (Clarkson from **Jonathan Weaver** and Davies) knocked out the Bison in the semi, but the Lightning struck a mortifying five times in the final before Clarkson and **Sam Zajac** put the Tigers on the board.

PLAYER AWARDS
Players' Player: **Jason Silverthorn**
Coach's Player: **Jason Silverthorn**
Most Valuable Player: **Doug Clarkson**
Best Forward: **Doug Clarkson**
Best Defenceman: **Sam Zajac**
Best Plus/Minus: **Matt Davies**
Most Improved Player: **Adam Taylor**
Combat Helmet (most MOMs): **Sam Gospel**

FACT FILE 2016-17
English Premier League: Winners
Play-offs: Finalists
Premier Cup: Semi-finalists

LEADING PLAYERS
Doug Clarkson *born 21 November 1988, Mimico, Ontario*
The giant 6ft 5in winger has a quick shot release that produced 56 goals in his 55 games. "And he's tremendous to have around the changing room," said coach Watkins.

Sam Gospel *born 27 March 1994, Nottingham*
Though technically only the back-up boy, his worth was recognised at the end of the season with the Combat Helmet for most Man of the Match nominations.

Jason Silverthorn *born 1 July 1979, Owen Sound, Ontario*
The veteran captain was an inspiration. "All young players should watch how he approaches the game, he's always prepared, physically and mentally," said his coach.

HISTORY: Founded 1985. Run by local businessmen after Telford Ice Sports Ltd was wound up in November 2016. **Leagues** EPIHL 2010-17, 2005-09; Brit. Nat'l Lge 1997-99; Premier League 1996/97; British League, Div One 1985-96. **Honours**: EPIHL 2016/17, 2014/15; English Challenge Cup 2014/15.

TELFORD TIGERS – PLAYER STATISTICS 2016/17

PLAYER	ENGLISH PREMIER					PLAY-OFFS				
Scorers	GP	G	A	Pts	Pim	GP	G	A	Pts	Pim
Doug Clarkson (I)	46	43	30	73	96	8	12	6	18	2
Matt Davies	42	16	63	79	54	8	0	10	10	2
Jason Silverthorn (I)	45	37	24	61	51	8	3	5	8	0
Milan Kolena (I)	44	29	25	54	123	8	1	3	4	2
Corey McEwen	47	22	23	45	37	8	4	6	10	0
Jonathan Weaver	31	7	32	39	12	8	4	7	11	2
Rick Plant	44	14	28	42	45	8	2	3	5	2
Sam Zajac	45	7	31	38	107	8	3	3	6	4
Lubomir Korhon (I)	22	8	14	22	6	8	1	4	5	10
Sam Oakford	42	2	23	25	14	8	0	2	2	10
Michal Satek (I) 4	22	9	17	26	10					
Adam Jones	47	3	12	15	38	8	1	2	3	20
Daniel Rose	46	4	10	14	24	8	1	3	4	2
Warren Tait	46	2	11	13	6	8	0	1	1	2
Adam Taylor	35	4	5	9	12	8	0	2	2	4
Daniel Scott 1	24	3	6	9	10					
Phil Hill 5	20	1	8	9	10					
Macaulay Heywood 3	21	4	4	8	22					
Gareth O'Flaherty 2	11	1	3	4	2	8	1	0	1	4
Joe Miller 1	15	2	2	n	18					
Corey Goodison	28	0	3	3	8	8	0	0	0	2
Joe Aston	25	0	2	2	0	8	0	0	0	0
Marcus Maynard 2	5	0	1	1	2					
Sam Gospel (N)	46	0	1	1	2	8	0	0	0	0
Jon Baston (I) (N)	19	0	0	0	0	8	0	0	0	2
Luke Brittle	8	0	0	0	2					
Ondrej Raszka (I) (N)	22	0	0	0	4					
Winning shots		2		2			0		0	
Bench penalties					22					4
TEAM TOTALS	48	220	378	594	737	8	33	57	90	74

	LEAGUE					PLAY OFFS				
Netminders	GP	Mins	SOG	GA	Sv%	GP	Mins	SOG	GA	Sv%
Jon Baston (I)	10	600	276	22	92.0	8	499	222	21	90.5
Ondrej Raszka (I)	17	1018	464	40	91.4					
Sam Gospel	21	1230	658	60	90.9	1	2	1	0	100.0
Winning shots			3					0		
Empty net goals			3	3				1	1	
TEAM TOTALS	48	2848	1401	128	90.9	8	501	224	22	90.2

Also appeared: *Brodie Jesson, Ted Thompson.*
Also played for: *1 Basingstoke Bison; 2 Hull Pirates; 3 Sheffield Steeldogs; 4 Guildford Flames; 5 Swindon Wildcats.*

Shutouts:
Baston (3) - league: 14 Jan at Bracknell Bees (28 saves); play-offs: 25 March v Peterborough Phantoms (25), 2 April v Sheffield Steeldogs (17).
Raszka -league: 27 Nov v Swindon Wildcats (29 saves).

English Premier League

Lightning Strikes Twice! Milton Keynes Lightning celebrate the play off final win against Telford Tigers (above – photo by Tony Sargent) and (below) MKL in action against Peterborough Phantoms in the home leg of the EPL Cup Final. (Photo by Lucy McGill)

(C) Lucy McGill Photography

English Premier League

ENGLISH PREMIER LEAGUE PLAY OFFS

EPL Play Off Final - Played at Coventry: 9th April 2017
Telford Tigers 2 – Milton Keynes Lightning 7

Semi Finals - Played 8th April 2017 at Coventry	
Guilford Flames 3	Basingstoke Bison 2
M/Keynes Lightning 8	Telford Tigers 3

EPL Play Offs Gp A	P	W	OW	OL	L	PIM	F	A	Pts
Guildford Flames	6	5	0	1	0	46	18	9	11
Telford Tigers	6	3	1	0	2	62	28	13	8
Peterborough Phantoms	6	3	0	0	3	48	26	19	6
Sheffield Steeldogs	6	0	0	0	6	85	8	39	0

EPL Play Offs Gp B	P	W	OW	OL	L	PIM	F	A	Pts
Basingstoke Bison	6	5	0	0	1	62	27	12	10
Milton Keynes Lightning	6	5	0	0	1	57	28	15	10
Swindon Wildcats	6	1	1	0	4	68	21	29	4
Hull Pirates	6	0	0	1	5	50	14	34	1

ENGLISH PREMIER LEAGUE CUP

EPL Cup Final - Played Over Two Legs Home & Away
Milton Keynes Lightning win 5-1 on aggregate

12th March 2017	18th March 2017
Peterborough Phantoms 2 - M/Keynes Lightning 1	M/Keynes Lightning 4 - Peterborough Phantoms 0

Semi Final 1	
Peterborough Phantoms win 11-4 on aggregate	
18th January 2017	22nd January 2017
Peterboro Phantoms 4	Telford Tigers 2
Telford Tigers 2	Peterboro Phantoms 7

Semi Final 2	
Milton Keynes Lightning win 11-3 on aggregate	
12th January 2017	15th January 2017
Hull Pirates 1 M/Keynes	M/Keynes Lightning 7
Lightning 4	Hull Pirates 2

EPL CUP TABLE	P	W	OW	OL	L	F	A	Pts
Telford Tigers	18	11	3	3	1	77	47	31
Milton Keynes Lightning	18	10	4	0	4	58	45	28
Hull Pirates	18	11	0	0	7	81	66	22
Peterborough Phantoms	18	8	2	1	7	76	54	21
Basingstoke Bison	18	10	0	1	7	54	40	21
Swindon Wildcats	18	7	2	2	7	59	54	20
Guildford Flames	18	8	0	3	7	63	63	19
Sheffield Steeldogs	18	6	1	2	9	58	64	16
Bracknell Bees	18	4	0	1	13	46	87	9
Manchester Phoenix	18	2	1	0	15	40	92	6

The first two league meetings between each pairing of teams also counted towards the cup group. The top four teams then went on to contest the semi-finals and final.

English Premier League

INTERVIEW: GREG BLAIS

We like to feature former players who gave good service to UK hockey and still reside over here and this time around we focus on former Wightlink Raiders and Hull Stingray netminder Greg Blais. Retired from the professional game now, NIHL South Editor Chris (Badger) Randall caught up with to see how life has been going for the Ontario - born goalie.

At what age did you first learn to skate?

I started skating from 3 years old. My Dad made me an outdoor rink in my garden. My mom and dad would take me on it. I used to push a chair around the ice.

How did you get into playing hockey?

I used to watch Hockey Night in Canada every Saturday night with my parents. I joined my first team at 4 years old. I was the goalie for my team from the very beginning.

What was the first league (senior) that you started playing?

At 16 I played junior A in Canada and then went on to Play NCAA College hockey in Boston. After my senior year of NCAA College hockey in Boston I went on to play with the Danbury Trashers in the United Hockey League. Danbury was my first professional team.

Who was responsible for getting you over to the UK and what were your first impressions?

My agent at the time was David Imonti and he got me to England. I had always wanted to play in England since I graduated from NCAA. As soon as I got to England I met Jason Coles who was my coach on the Isle of Wight. Ha ha - my first impression of the Island was I could not believe how small the rink was and that a professional team played on it.

I have a lot of good memories playing on the island. It's too bad now that the ice rink is closed. Hockey was a huge part of the Island. I feel sorry for everyone on the island that they lost their rink. Losing the rink affected my children as they would not be able to play hockey and follow in their dad's footsteps.

English Premier League

You eventually stepped up to the Elite League .. what was that experience like ?

My goal had been to play at Elite League level and I played for the Hull stingrays, which was a great experience. I am good friends with the coach at the time Sylvain Cloutier as we come from the same hometown - Sault Ste Marie in Canada. I found the standard similar to the French Magnus League but more American style of playing. The standard of the Elite UK is very good. My first year in the Elite League was the NHL lockout year so we had a few good NHL players join. It was pretty exciting playing against Redwings forward Drew Miller as, at the time, he played for the Braehead Clan.

You played in some other countries ? Where was that and what was that experience like ?

I played in Norway for the Bergen Flyers. I really enjoyed playing in Norway. The travel was amazing as Norway is such a beautiful country. I also had an opportunity to play in Belgium and Holland but while I was in Holland unfortunately my team went bankrupt half way through the season.

Since you retired, what do you miss most from no longer playing ?

I miss everything about playing. I miss the team bonding in the locker room especially, but there is nothing like getting ready for a game before the first puck drop.

When you retired from playing professionally what career path did you take ?

As soon as I left the game, I joined the Surrey Police force as a first responder. I absolutely love it. I work as a team and we all work hard together - just like in ice hockey. II wish I joined Surrey Police sooner than I did in 2015 but it was hard to pick a time to retire from the game I love and played since the young age of 3. I met some good friends in Surrey and now my life is in the Surrey Area. I would definitely recommend people that are looking for an amazing career to visit www.surrey.police.uk/jobs.

I enjoy going to work everyday as I never know what to expect as everyday is different. I love to help people when they need it and make people's lives better when I can.

Is there a police team?

Yes, Surrey Police have a hockey team. I played a few games with them for fun and attended practices. For the past year I been focusing on my children and my girlfriend Michelle so I have been finding it hard to find the time to play. This coming season I will be playing a lot more with the Surrey Police team. They are a great bunch of guys and it is always a good feeling stepping on the ice again.

Do your team mates give you the banter or treat you differently being a former top level netminder? Or are you just one of the guys?

The guys don't treat me differently and I wouldn't want them to. I was lucky to have played at the level that I did but I would never want to be treated better than anyone else. I will always just be one of the guys just playing a game.

I recall an EPL game between the Wightlink Raiders (your team at the time) and the visiting Slough Jets. A clapper from close range from team import/owner/player Zoran Kosic catching you pretty good, resulting in your equipment having to be cut free. The island fans clubbed together to get you new gear - what does that tell you about British hockey fans?

Yes I remember that game well. I was taken off the ice on a stretcher and sent to St Mary's Hospital. I could not believe how much support the Isle of Wight Raiders had. I never been treated like that before and I couldn't believe they raised funds to buy new equipment.

I played on a number of teams in the Elite/EPL level and I found the British hockey fans to be amazing. They really support their teams. It was always amazing playing in England. No matter what team I played for or what team I was playing against the fan support was incredible. When I joined a new team the fans were always very nice and supportive.

English Premier League

Above right: Greg Blais at EPL Telford Tigers - season 2011/12 (Photo by Steve Brodie)

Above: Blais with fellow netminder Ben Bowns at Hull Stingrays in the 2012/13 EIHL season. (photographer to be confirmed)

Left: Blais at Peterborough Phantoms in the 2014/15 EPL season – his last before retiring. Photo by Tom Scott / AMO Images)

Below: In action for Hull against Dundee Stars in the Elite League. (Photo by Derek Black – www.centre-ice.co.uk)

NIHL North - Moralee Conference

Top Photo: Stuart Kerr of the Solway Sharks receives his Moralee Conference winner's medal from Liz and Mary Moralee, daughter and widow of Neville Moralee, after whom the Conference is named (Solway Sharks)
Above Left: Top points scorer Scott McKenzie of Dragons IHC (Photo by Peter Sheffield – www.psd-images.com)
Above Right: Top netminder Calum Hepburn of Solway Sharks (Duncan Speirs)

NIHL North - Moralee Conference

Final League Table – Moralee Conference 2016/17

Team	P	W	D	L	F	A	+/-	PIM	Pts
Solway Sharks	28	23	3	2	134	52	82	232	49
Billingham Stars	28	18	0	10	135	105	30	311	36
Blackburn Hawks	28	12	2	14	108	125	-17	517	26
Solihull Barons	28	11	2	15	117	122	-5	515	24
Whitley Warriors	28	12	2	14	107	118	-11	455	24*
Sutton Sting	28	9	3	16	83	106	-23	236	21
Deeside Dragons	28	9	3	16	114	153	-39	278	21
Telford Tigers	28	9	3	16	107	124	-17	685	21

Whitley Warriors forfeit game at Telford Tigers on 3rd December 2016 after refusing to play the third period. Tigers were leading 5-0 at the time and the result was allowed to stand. Warriors also had 2 points deducted.

Leading Points Scorers - Moralee Conference 2016/17

Player	Team	GP	G	A	Pts	PIM
Scott McKenzie	Deeside Dragons	25	19	34	53	16
Richard Bentham	B'Hawks & Solway	23	25	27	52	44
Chris Sykes	Billingham Stars	25	23	28	51	12
Dennis Bostrum	Billingham Stars	28	29	16	45	24
Aaron Davies	Blackburn Hawks	28	20	22	42	26
Karol Jets	Telford Tigers	25	19	23	42	38
Dean Holland	Whitley Warriors	28	19	22	41	54
Joe Henry	Solihull Barons	26	15	24	39	71
Lloyd Gibson	Sutton Sting	24	19	18	37	20
Steven Moore	Solway Sharks	27	11	26	37	0
Niklas Ottosson	Solihull Barons	26	15	22	37	12
Callum Watson	Whitley Warriors	26	20	17	37	32

Top Netminders – Moralee Conference 2016/17

Netminder	Team	GP	SA	GA	Sv%	SO
Calum Hepburn	Solway Sharks	20	613	34	94.45%	1
Dmitri Zimozdra	Sutton Sting	23	1010	76	92.48%	0
James Flavell	Billingham Stars	26	948	83	91.24%	0
Stuart Lee Ashton	Blackburn Hawks	27	923	86	90.68%	0
Joshua Nicholls	Solihull Barons	19	580	56	90.34%	0
Jonah Armstrong	Deeside Dragons	15	382	39	89.79%	0
Zack Brown	Sutton Sting	23	247	26	89.47%	1
Richard Lawson	Whitley Warriors	28	907	98	89.20%	1
Daniel Brittle	Telford Tigers	28	994	108	89.13%	1

NIHL North 2016/17
Moralee Conference Review
by Chris Mackenzie

The 2016/17 season got underway in early September with 8 teams battling it out for honours in the division. The Champions of NIHL North in the previous season the Blackburn Hawks saw much of their playing squad and coaching set up change during the close season with former Sutton Sting Head Coach Matt Darlow now running the Hawks bench.

Once the action got underway it soon became clear that the Solway Sharks were one of the leading contenders for the title in 2016/17 as Martin Grubb's side only loss in their early season match ups was a cup defeat to Blackburn.

Sharks looked to build their success on an extremely strong defence with imports Juraj Senko, Kim Miettinen and the experienced Brit James Hutchinson patrolling the Solway blue line.

Billingham Stars' Dennis Böstrom was the highest goal scorer in the Moralee Conference with 29 in 28 games. (Photo by Carol White - Stars Media)

Newcomers to the division the Deeside Dragons were also enjoying some fine results in their opening games of the term as the Dragons led by player/coach Scott McKenzie picked up positive results against the likes of the Telford Tigers, Solihull Barons and Sutton Sting.

Reigning Champions the Blackburn Hawks started the season in mixed form and the Hawks organisation opted to replace their highly regarded and recently appointed Head Coach Matt Darlow with player Steve Duncombe. This move shocked many observers as Darlow was given little time to become accustomed to his new surroundings before the club dispensed with his services.

As the table started to take shape it became clear that Solway were the form team in the league that every other side would be looking to catch. Every team in the division had realistic play off ambitions given just how competitive the league was when any of the teams placed from 2nd to 8th could get the better of one another on any given night.

Solway's mean defence and ruthless offence saw them win every one of their league games until early December when they went down to a 3-2 defeat on the road against the Billingham Stars on Teesside.

NIHL North - Moralee Conference

Stars import forward Dennis Bostrum impressed as he grabbed 2 of his sides goals however a mention must also be given to Billingham netminder James Flavell who was able to record a save percentage of 95% in the match up.

Billingham themselves had been in mixed form early on in the campaign, however their victory over Solway came when they were in fine form as Stars won 6 of the 7 league games they played during November and December which saw Terry Ward's side take a more prominent place in the league standings.

The fight for play-off spots for all of the sides in the division remained tight however Whitley Warriors were dealt a blow to their hopes of a top 4 finish when they were docked 2 points by the league for leaving the ice during their away game against the Telford Tigers in December.

Solway maintained their superb form all season long and Martin Grubb's side led by skipper Struan Tonnar managed to accumulate 49 points during the course of the season to comfortably secure the title. Billingham took the honours of league runners up as they ended the season with 36 points ensuring they qualified for the play offs by a healthy margin.

The final 2 play spots went down to the wire with the Blackburn Hawks and Solihull Barons only securing their play-off participation in the final stages of the campaign. Whitley Warriors ended the term level on points with the Barons however Solihull's better head to head record saw Perry Doyle's side qualify for finals weekend. Warriors points deduction proving crucial as the Tynesiders missed out on that final play-off spot.

The final 3 sides in the table the Sutton Sting, Deeside Dragons and Telford Tigers all finished level on 21 points, with Telford finishing bottom of the mini league they were relegated to Division 2 of the Northern set up. Deeside took on the Widnes Wild (who had finished 2nd in Division 2) in a promotion/relegation play-off match up, Dragons came out on top 4-3 in a tight game with Jordan Bannon grabbing 2 of Deeside's goals.

Play off final weekend saw Solway take on Solihull and Billingham take on Blackburn at Ice Sheffield. Sharks got the better of the Barons in a tight affair by 3 goals to 2 before Hawks were beaten 7-3 by the Stars in a entertaining goal-fest. The final saw Solway edge it by 3 goals to 1 with Sharks netminder Callum Hepburn impressing everyone who was in attendance with some smart stops and a save percentage of over 96% for the Scottish side.

Coach of the Year – Martin Grubb (Solway Sharks)
Player of the Year – Rick Bentham (Blackburn Hawks)
Young Player of the Year – Jordan Buesa (Solway Sharks)

All Star Team of the Year :
NM – Dmitri Zimozdra (Sutton Sting)
D – Juraj Senko (Solway Sharks) Kim Miettinen (Solway Sharks)
F – Rick Bentham (Blackburn Hawks) Dennis Bostrum (Billingham Stars) Chris Sykes (Billingham Stars)

NIHL North - Moralee Conference

Billingham Stars – Player Statistics – 2016/17

Player	Regular Season					Play Offs				
	GP	G	A	Pts	PIM	GP	G	A	Pts	PIM
Chris Sykes	25	23	28	51	12	2	2	2	4	4
Dennis Bostrum	28	29	16	45	24	2	0	0	0	2
Callum Davies	25	9	25	34	8	2	1	2	3	0
Michael Elder	28	16	18	34	22	2	2	1	3	2
Daniel Palmebjork	28	12	21	33	4	2	2	1	3	2
Jack Watkins	27	18	12	30	8	2	1	2	3	2
Michael Bowman	27	13	15	28	8	2	0	0	0	0
James Moss	20	5	10	15	6	2	0	2	2	2
Richie Thornton	26	0	13	13	28	2	0	0	0	0
Thomas Keeley	21	1	7	8	20	2	0	2	2	0
Scott Ward	24	1	7	8	14	2	0	0	0	0
Jack Emerson	26	3	4	7	4	2	0	0	0	0
Andy Finn	23	0	6	6	8	2	0	1	1	2
Benjamin Davison	17	3	1	4	18	2	0	1	1	0
Ross Hanlon	14	0	4	4	26	2	0	0	0	0
Luke Brown	13	1	2	3	8	2	0	0	0	29
Matthew Campbell	17	1	2	3	6	0	0	0	0	0
Joshua Nertney	22	0	1	1	12	2	0	0	0	0
Billy Isaac Nicholson	7	0	1	1	2	0	0	0	0	0
Scott Cooper	15	0	0	0	10	2	0	0	0	0
Jack Davies	7	0	0	0	24	0	0	0	0	0
James Flavell	26	0	0	0	4	2	0	0	0	0
Benjamin Gill	1	0	0	0	0	0	0	0	0	0
Callum Read	12	0	0	0	31	0	0	0	0	0
Callum Reynolds	4	0	0	0	0	0	0	0	0	0
William Robson	16	0	0	0	2	0	0	0	0	0
Mark Watson	24	0	0	0	0	2	0	0	0	0
Paul Windridge	1	0	0	0	0	0	0	0	0	0

Billingham Stars - Netminder Statistics - 2016/17

Netminder	Regular Season					Play Offs				
	GP	SA	GA	Sv%	SO	GP	SA	GA	Sv%	SO
James Flavell	26	948	83	91.24%	0	2	89	6	93.15	0
Mark Watson	24	184	21	88.59%	0	0	0	0	0	0

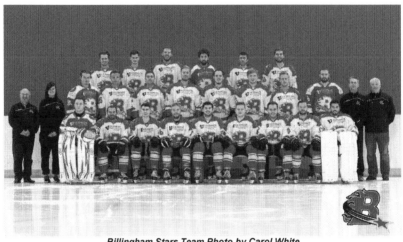

Billingham Stars Team Photo by Carol White

Back row: Billy Nicholson, Jack Emerson, Tom Keeley, Michael Bowman, Paul Windridge, Ben Davison
Middle row: Terry Ward (Director of Coaching), Sadie Lee Pinchbeck (Physiotherapist), Jack Watkins, Jack Davies, Richie Thornton, Dennis Boström, James Moss, Will Robson, Luke Brown, Callum Read, Allen Flavell (General Manager), Steve Campbell (Equipment Manager). Front row: Ben Gill, Scott Ward, Josh Nertney, Scott Cooper, Michael Elder, Callum Davies, Chris Sykes, Daniel Palmebjörk, James Flavell

Blackburn Hawks Team Photo by John Milton

NIHL North - Moralee Conference

Blackburn Hawks – Player Statistics – 2016/17

Player	Regular Season					Play Offs				
	GP	G	A	Pts	PIM	GP	G	A	Pts	PIM
Richard Bentham	20	25	27	52	44	1	0	1	1	12
Aaron Davies	28	20	22	42	26	1	1	0	1	0
Steven Duncombe	28	2	23	25	65	1	0	0	0	2
Mikko Sierman	26	10	14	24	14	1	0	0	0	0
Jozef Istocy	15	15	8	23	29	1	1	0	1	0
Philip Mulcahy	27	9	14	23	18	1	0	0	0	0
James Riddoch	28	6	13	19	8	1	0	1	1	0
Nicholas A. Oliver	26	6	11	17	90	1	0	0	0	0
Corey Stones	19	5	5	10	56	1	0	0	0	2
Robert Streetly	28	1	8	9	14	1	0	1	1	0
Lewis Baldwin	6	4	4	8	2	0	0	0	0	0
Patrik Nyman	6	4	4	8	16	0	0	0	0	0
Thomas Parkinson	25	2	4	6	2	1	1	0	1	0
Bobby Caunce	8	2	2	4	6	0	0	0	0	0
Oliver Lomax	15	1	3	4	30	1	0	0	0	4
Reece Cairney-Witter	27	0	3	3	42	1	0	0	0	0
Chris Gee	16	0	3	3	18	1	0	0	0	0
James Royds	9	0	3	3	2	1	0	1	1	0
Carl Price	24	1	1	2	14	1	0	0	0	0
Stuart Lee Ashton	27	0	1	1	27	1	0	0	0	0
Christopher Butler	19	0	1	1	22	1	0	0	0	0
Harry James Mercer	11	0	1	1	0	1	0	0	0	0
Daniel Sanderson	11	0	1	1	0	1	0	0	0	0
Kyle Haslam	8	0	0	0	0	0	0	0	0	0
Christopher Jones	1	0	0	0	0	0	0	0	0	0
Sean Jones	1	0	0	0	0	0	0	0	0	0
Craig Lutkevitch	2	0	0	0	0	0	0	0	0	0
Daniel Morris	2	0	0	0	0	0	0	0	0	0
Niks Trapans	26	0	0	0	0	1	0	0	0	0

Blackburn Hawks - Netminder Statistics – 2016/17

Netminder	Regular Season					Play Offs				
	GP	SA	GA	Sv%	SO	GP	SA	GA	Sv%	SO
Stuart Lee Ashton	27	923	86	90.68%	0	1	41	7	82.93	0
Niks Trapans	26	301	39	87.04%	0	0	0	0	0	0

Dragons (Deeside) – Player Statistics – 2016/17

	Moralee					Promotion				
	GP	G	A	Pts	PIM	GP	G	A	Pts	PIM
Scott McKenzie	25	19	34	53	16	1	0	2	2	4
James Parsons	27	19	16	35	18	1	1	0	1	0
Filip Supa	23	19	14	33	12	1	1	1	2	0
Markus Kankaanranta	18	15	14	29	6	0	0	0	0	0
Ross Kennedy	21	4	13	17	22	1	0	0	0	2
Matthew Wainwright	28	1	13	14	4	1	0	1	1	0
Jordan Bannon	11	8	5	13	12	1	2	0	2	2
Simon Furnival	26	3	10	13	26	1	0	0	0	25
Geoff Wigglesworth	24	6	7	13	20	1	0	1	1	0
Corey Stones	4	5	5	10	56	0	0	0	0	0
Andrew Chappell	27	2	7	9	6	1	0	0	0	0
Marc Lovell	24	1	7	8	24	1	0	0	0	0
Alex Parry	14	5	3	8	10	1	0	0	0	4
Bradley Betteridge	4	2	4	6	20	0	0	0	0	0
Ryan Kemp	27	5	1	6	0	1	0	0	0	0
Gavin Austin	27	0	5	5	14	1	0	0	0	0
Chris Gee	11	0	3	3	18	0	0	0	0	0
Jacob Heron	1	1	2	3	0	0	0	0	0	0
Matthew Barlow	3	1	1	2	0	0	0	0	0	0
Peter Gazda	5	1	1	2	6	0	0	0	0	0
Ryan David Jones	28	1	1	2	22	1	0	0	0	12
Joshua Richardson	16	0	2	2	0	1	0	0	0	0
Cain David Taylor	4	2	0	2	2	0	0	0	0	0
Steven Fellows	7	0	1	1	2	0	0	0	0	0
Jordan Fisher	3	0	1	1	0	0	0	0	0	0
Kenneth Williams	11	0	1	1	2	0	0	0	0	0
Jonah Armstrong	15	0	0	0	0	0	0	0	0	0
Denis Bell	9	0	0	0	0	1	0	0	0	0
Michael Clancy	15	0	0	0	0	0	0	0	0	0
Matthew Compton	25	0	0	0	0	0	0	0	0	0
Scott Egerton	6	0	0	0	0	0	0	0	0	0
Joseph Hazeldine	1	0	0	0	0	1	0	2	2	2
Jacob Lutwyche	1	0	0	0	2	1	0	0	0	0
Louis Morgan	10	0	0	0	10	1	0	0	0	0
Billy Perks	2	0	0	0	0	1	0	0	0	0
Ashley Paul Smith	4	0	0	0	0	0	0	0	0	0
Macauley Stones	1	0	0	0	6	0	0	0	0	0

Dragons (Deeside) – Netminder Statistics – 2016/17

	Moralee					Promotion			
Netminder	GP	SA	GA	SA%	SO	GP	SA	GA	SA%
Jonah Armstrong	15	382	39	89.79%	0	0	0	0	0
Denis Bell	9	322	40	87.58%	0	1	33	3	90.91
Ashley Paul Smith	4	169	22	86.98%	0	0	0	0	0
Matthew Compton	25	345	49	85.80%	0	0	0	0	0

NIHL North - Moralee Conference

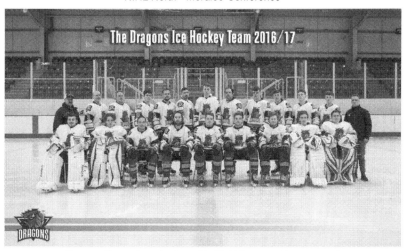

Dragons Team photo by Peter Sheffield (www.psd-images.com)

Back Row (left to right): Bruce Morton, Scott Egerton, Geoff Wigglesworth, Ryan Kemp, Filip Supa, Simon Furnival, Josh Richardson, Gavin Austin, Ryan Jones, Louis Morgan, Ross Kennedy, Michael Clancy, Charles Humphries (Equip Mgr)

Front Row (left to right): Denis Bell, Ethan Armstrong, Andrew Chappell, Scott McKenzie, James Parsons, Marc Lovell, Matt Wainwright, Jonah Armstrong, Matt Compton

Solihull Barons Team Photo (credit: Steve Crampton)

Back row l-r: Gary Rogers (Equipment), Erin Dobbey (Physio), Tomas Janak, Kieran Papps, Brandon Anderton, James Moeller, Matt Maurice, Dale White, Jacob Smith, Paul Davies, Tom Soar, Richard Crowe, Andy Whitehouse, Niklas Ottosson, Ed Eaton, Kelly Woolley (Physio)

Front row l-r: Sam Hewitt, Rich Slater, Phil Knight, Dave Rogers, Perry Doyle, Ian Lewis (Management), Josh Bruce, Joe Henry, Ryan Selwood, Josh Nicholls

NIHL North - Moralee Conference

Solihull Barons – Player Statistics - 2016/17

	Regular Season					Play Offs				
	GP	G	A	Pts	PIM	GP	G	A	Pts	PIM
Joe Henry	26	15	24	39	71	1	0	1	1	0
Niklas Ottosson	26	15	22	37	12	1	0	0	0	0
Thomas Soar	25	18	16	34	6	1	0	0	0	0
Josh Bruce	20	10	19	29	89	1	1	1	2	2
Matthew Maurice	27	16	12	28	20	1	0	0	0	0
Tomas Janak	23	5	17	22	24	1	0	1	1	2
Andrew Whitehouse	28	6	12	18	31	1	1	0	1	0
Richard Slater	24	11	6	17	10	1	0	0	0	0
Edward James Eaton	15	3	10	13	12	0	0	0	0	0
Ryan Selwood	25	3	9	12	28	1	0	0	0	2
Richard James Crowe	28	2	6	8	24	1	0	0	0	2
David Rogers	22	2	6	8	24	1	0	0	0	0
Elliot Rhys Farrell	28	3	4	7	27	1	0	0	0	0
Dale White	14	4	2	6	36	0	0	0	0	0
Phil Knight	19	2	3	5	41	1	0	0	0	0
Paul Davies	9	1	3	4	2	0	0	0	0	0
Perry Doyle	5	0	2	2	32	0	0	0	0	0
Kieran Papps	28	1	1	2	0	1	0	0	0	0
Jacob Charles Smith	25	0	2	2	0	0	0	0	0	0
Brandon Anderton	11	1	0	1	2	1	0	0	0	0
Stuart Clayton	13	0	1	1	6	0	0	0	0	0
Sam Hewitt	20	0	1	1	0	1	0	0	0	0
Michelle Franklin	2	0	0	0	0	0	0	0	0	0
Stephen James Heape	6	0	0	0	6	0	0	0	0	0
James Robert Moeller	15	0	0	0	0	1	0	0	0	0
Joshua Nicholls	19	0	0	0	10	1	0	0	0	0
Connor George Ranby	8	0	0	0	0	0	0	0	0	0

Solihull Barons – Netminder Statistics - 2016/17

	Regular Season					Play Offs				
	GP	SA	GA	Sa%	SO	GP	Time	SA	GA	Sa%
Connor Ranby	8	81	7	91.36%	0	0	0	0	0	0
Joshua Nicholls	19	580	56	90.34%	0	1	60.42	49	3	93.88
Sam Hewitt	20	533	58	89.12%	0	0	0	0	0	0
Empty Net	0	0	0	0	0	1	0.23	4	0	100.00

NIHL North - Moralee Conference

Solway Sharks – Player Statistics - 2016/17

	Regular Season					Play Offs				
	GP	G	A	Pts	PIM	GP	G	A	Pts	PIM
Steven Moore	27	11	26	37	0	2	0	2	2	0
Kim Miettinen	27	9	25	34	10	2	1	1	2	2
Daniel Abercrombie	27	20	11	31	8	2	1	0	1	0
Joe Coulter	27	6	21	27	4	2	0	2	2	4
Connor Henderson	19	9	18	27	12	2	0	2	2	0
Duncan Speirs	19	13	14	27	8	2	1	1	2	0
Struan Tonnar	25	18	9	27	24	2	1	1	2	0
Jordan Buesa	18	8	17	25	18	0	0	0	0	0
Juraj Senko	26	9	15	24	2	2	1	0	1	0
Marc Fowley	19	8	10	18	10	2	0	0	0	2
Ross Murray	22	3	13	16	67	2	0	0	0	0
James Hutchinson	26	3	10	13	8	2	0	1	1	0
Stuart Andrews	25	2	6	8	29	2	0	0	0	4
Stuart Kerr	27	2	6	8	2	2	0	0	0	0
Ben Edmonds	18	3	4	7	2	2	0	0	0	0
Scott Henderson	18	3	2	5	8	2	1	0	1	0
Richard Bentham	4	4	1	5	4	0	0	0	0	0
Nathan Britton	1	3	0	3	0	0	0	0	0	0
Darren Stattersfield	9	0	3	3	10	0	0	0	0	0
Elliot Kinell	1	0	2	2	0	0	0	0	0	0
James Wallace	4	0	2	2	2	0	0	0	0	0
Alexander Harding	1	0	1	1	2	0	0	0	0	0
Kieran Hobbins	4	0	1	1	0	0	0	0	0	0
Callum Blair	1	0	0	0	0	0	0	0	0	0
Kieran Hair	6	0	0	0	0	0	0	0	0	0
Calum Hepburn	20	0	0	0	0	2	0	0	0	0
Kyle Johnston	2	0	0	0	0	0	0	0	0	0
Tom Johnston	1	0	0	0	0	0	0	0	0	0
Chris Rae	22	0	0	0	0	2	0	0	0	0
Richard Thorpe	1	0	0	0	0	0	0	0	0	0

Solway Sharks – Netminder Statistics - 2016/17

	Regular Season					Play Offs				
	GP	SA	GA	Sa%	SO	GP	Time	SA	GA	Sa%
Calum Hepburn	20	613	34	94.45%	1	2	121.05	60	3	95.00
Kieran Hobbins	4	117	7	94.02%	1	0	0	0	0	0
Chris Rae	22	96	11	88.54%	2	0	0	0	0	0

Solway Sharks Team Photo by Duncan Speirs

Back Row: Hazel Mair, Connor Henderson, Stewart Kerr, Joe Coulter, Stevie Moore, Daniel Abercrombie, Scott Houston. / Middle Row: John Little, Les Maxwell, Kim Miettinen, Rick Bentham, Calum Hepburn, Jurai Senko, Duncan Speirs, James Wallace, Scott McMeekan, Rab Murray. / Front Row: Marc Fowley, James Hutchinson, Kieran Hobbins, Martin Grubb, Struan Tonnar, Chris Rae, Ross Murray, Stuart Andrews

Sutton Sting Team Group by Keith & Jenny Davies

Left to Right: Dimitri Zimozdra, Dave Pyatt, James Goodman, Simon Butterworth, Nick Winters, Brady Doxy, Jamie Spurr, Scott Morris, Cam Glasby, Chris Wilcox, Matt Jeffcock, Elliot Meadows, Oliver Mitchell, Joe Colton, Charlie Thompson, Mark Turner, Ryan Johnson, Scott Glover, Tom Barry.

NIHL North - Moralee Conference

Sutton Sting – Player Statistics - 2016/17

Player	GP	G	A	Pts	PIM
Lloyd Gibson	24	19	18	37	20
Joseph Colton	26	12	21	33	2
James Spurr	27	14	17	31	10
Ryan Johnson	22	9	9	18	38
Charles Thompson	16	10	7	17	2
Chris Wilcox	28	2	14	16	8
Scott Morris	24	3	12	15	14
Simon Butterworth	9	2	5	7	0
James Goodman	26	3	4	7	80
Mark Turner	24	4	3	7	2
Brady Doxey	21	1	2	3	2
Matt Jeffcock	26	1	2	3	4
Benjamin Jones	26	1	2	3	12
Oliver Mitchell	21	2	1	3	2
Charlie Saunders	25	0	3	3	8
Martin Finkes	8	0	2	2	4
David Pyatt	17	0	2	2	6
Thomas Barry	6	0	1	1	4
Jordan Fisher	2	0	1	1	0
Scott Glover	7	0	1	1	0
Elliot Meadows	20	0	1	1	0
Dmitri Zimozdra	23	0	1	1	10
Zack Brown	23	0	0	0	0
Cameron Glasby	20	0	0	0	0
Thomas Marshall	2	0	0	0	0
Jamie Scott	16	0	0	0	2
Craig Wallis	2	0	0	0	0
Nicholas Winters	1	0	0	0	0

Sutton Sting – Netminder Statistics - 2016/17

Netminder	GP	SA	GA	Sa%	SO
Dmitri Zimozdra	23	1010	76	92.48%	0
Zack Brown	23	247	26	89.47%	1

NIHL North - Moralee Conference

Telford Tigers – Player Statistics - 2016/17

Player	GP	G	A	Pts	PIM
Karol Jets	25	19	23	42	38
Adam Brittle	24	17	17	34	42
Matthew Viney	27	13	19	32	36
Luke Brittle	22	9	17	26	56
Callum Bowley	19	8	15	23	16
Joseph Lee Aston	15	4	9	13	8
Daniel Mackriel	23	4	8	12	56
Ben Simister	21	5	6	11	34
James Smith	13	5	6	11	14
Corey Goodison	12	4	4	8	10
Conor Gordon	24	4	3	7	74
Simon Harrison	23	5	2	7	24
Daniel Harrison	24	3	4	7	32
Bradley Betteridge	8	2	4	6	20
Joshua Hustwick	27	1	5	6	36
Dale White	6	4	2	6	36
Daniel Croft	28	0	5	5	28
Callum Kurt Griffin	22	2	2	4	10
Matthew Price	20	0	2	2	2
Benjamin Washburn	25	1	1	2	6
Joseph Gilbert	8	0	1	1	4
Owen Bennett	15	0	0	0	38
Daniel Brittle	28	0	0	0	93
Louis Edwards	26	0	0	0	0
Michael Gilbert	1	0	0	0	0
Brodie Ian Jesson	7	0	0	0	0
Jake Nurse	1	0	0	0	0
William Reed	9	0	0	0	0
Edward (Ted) Thompson	1	0	0	0	0

Telford Tigers – Netminder Statistics 2016/17

Netminder	GP	SA	GA	Sv%	SO
Daniel Brittle	28	994	108	89.13%	1
Louis Edwards	26	80	16	80.00%	1

NIHL North - Moralee Conference

Telford Tigers Team Group Photo by Keith & Jenny Davies

Back Row: Martin Price, Owen Bennett, Dan Harrison, Callum Griffin, Conor Gordon, Daniel Brittle, Simon Harrison, Dan Mackriel, Adam Brittle, Luke Brittle, Dale White, Daniel Croft, Ben Washburn, Callum Bowley, Mike Washburn, Jason Parry
Front Row: Joe Gilbert, Will Reed, James Smith, Joshua Hustwick, Ben Simister, Matt Viney, Karol jets, Louis Edwards

Whitley Warriors Team Photo by Colin Lawson

Back Row: Lee Ross (kit man) Liam Smedley, Ross Douglass, Andre Payette, Dan Pye, Jordan Barnes, Niall Simpson, Lawson Glasby
Middle Row: Anthony Wetherall, Liam Brown, Craig Johnson, Jamie Ord, Josh Maddock, Ben Richards, DJ Good,
Front Row: Jordan Boyle, Dave Holland (assistant coach) Callum Watson, Martin Crammond, Richie Lawson, Dean Holland, Shaun Kippin, David Longstaff (player/coach), Rory Dunn

NIHL North - Moralee Conference

Whitley Warriors – Player Statistics 2016/17

Player	GP	G	A	Pts	PIM
Dean Holland	28	19	22	41	54
Callum Watson	26	20	17	37	32
David Longstaff	26	7	26	33	28
Daniel Good	28	10	19	29	10
Jordan Barnes	26	10	15	25	42
Shaun Kippin	27	11	13	24	26
Harry Harley	21	9	13	22	6
Ben Richards	14	4	4	8	2
Daniel Pye	20	3	4	7	14
Martin Crammond	28	0	6	6	20
Lawson Glasby	28	5	1	6	4
Andre Payette	20	2	4	6	153
Craig Johnson	28	0	5	5	16
Joe Stamp	13	1	4	5	4
Josh Maddock	26	0	4	4	16
Liam Brown	11	0	2	2	2
Jamie Ord	3	1	1	2	0
Niall Simpson	27	1	1	2	4
Liam Smedley	27	0	2	2	6
Stuart Tomlinson	11	2	0	2	0
Anthony Wetherell	11	1	1	2	2
Alan Yarrow	14	1	0	1	4
Jordan Boyle	16	0	0	0	0
Alistair Brummitt	1	0	0	0	0
Ross Douglass	17	0	0	0	0
Rory Dunn	12	0	0	0	0
Richard Lawson	28	0	0	0	0

Whitley Warriors – Netminder Statistics - 2016/17

Netminder	GP	SA	GA	Sa%	SO
Richard Lawson	28	907	98	89.20%	1
Jordan Boyle	16	93	13	86.02%	1
Rory Dunn	12	19	4	78.95%	0

NIHL North – North Cup

NIHL NORTH CUP

Solway Sharks' captain Struan Tonnar receives the NIHL North cup from the EIHA's Charles Dacres
Photo by David Morrison.
(www.david-morrison-photography.co.uk)

The Solway Sharks secured the NIHL North Cup after a 6-3 home win over Whitley Warriors on 21st January which meant that they couldn't be overtaken by anyone else in the Cup group, despite the other teams all having cup games still to play.

The Sharks' only defeat in the competition came away at Blackburn in their first cup game in September. Because teams had already agreed their league fixtures before the cup was announced, some cup games were also played as league games – but with the cup game results in the case of draw being decided by a period of sudden death over-time and points being awarded for overtime wins and losses.

3 points were awarded for an outright win in the Cup competition, 2 for an overtime win in the case of a draw and 1 for an overtime loss.

Sharks' Kim Miettenen (3+13) and Duncan Speirs (7+9) were the top points scorers in the Cup with 16 points each, although Blackburn Hawks Aaron Davies was the top goal scorer with 10 goals to which he added assists.

The cup was presented by EIHA vice president Charles Dacres after the Sharks' last home game of the season in Dumfries – a 10-0 victory over Blackburn in their last cup game on 25th March 2017.

NIHL North Cup 2016/17

Team	GP	W	OW	OL	L	PIM	F	A	Pts
Solway Sharks	12	10	1	0	1	144	78	31	32
Billingham Stars	12	4	1	1	6	99	49	59	15
Blackburn Hawks	12	4	0	1	7	354	37	60	13
Whitley Warriors	12	4	0	0	8	242	43	57	12

NIHL North - Moralee Conference

Above: Solway Sharks celebrate their treble trophy win after the Play Off final (Photo by Duncan Speirs)
Below left: Sharks in action in the final v Billingham Stars and the Semi Final v Solihull Barons. Below right:
Receiving the trophy from EIHA Vice President Charles Dacres (All photos by Duncan Speirs)

NIHL North - Moralee Conference

Sunday 9th April 2017 – Play Off Final
Solway Sharks 3 – Billingham Stars 1 (at iceSheffield)
Period Scores: 0-0, 1-0, 2-1
Shots On Goal: Sharks 48 – Stars 31 (16-8, 9-12, 23-11)
Penalties In Minutes: Sharks 6 – Stars 14

Sharks Scoring: Daniel Abercrombie, Juraj Senko & Scott Henderson all 1+0, Joe Coulter, Connor Henderson, Duncan Speirs, Kim Miettinen, Struan Tonnar all 0+1

Stars Scoring: Callum Davies 1+0, Michael Elder & James Moss both 0+1

Sharks Players: *Stuart Kerr, Daniel Abercrombie, Joe Coulter, Juraj Senko, Chris Rae, Stuart Andrews, Ben Edmonds, Connor Henderson, Calum Hepburn, Marc Fowley, Duncan Speirs, Kim Miettinen, Struan Tonnar, James Hutchinson, Steven Moore, Scott Henderson, Ross Murray*

Stars Players: *Joshua Nertney, James Moss, Scott Ward, Andy Finn, James Flavell, Chris Sykes, Michael Bowman, Richie Thornton, Benjamin Davison, Luke Brown, Mark Watson, Jack Emerson, Scott Cooper, Ross Hanlon, Michael Elder, Callum Davies, Thomas Keeley, Daniel Jimmy Palmebjork, Dennis Bostrum, Jack Watkins*

Match Officials: David Farren - Referee, Haydn Hunter - Linesman, Samuel Campbell - Linesman

Saturday 8th April 2017 – Play Off Semi Final
Solway Sharks 3 – Solihull Barons 2 (OTW)
Period Scores: 1-1, 0-1, 1-0, 1-0
Shots On Goal: Sharks 53 – Barons 29 (17-6, 17-14, 11-9, 4-0)
Penalties In Minutes: Sharks 6 – Barons 8

Sharks Scoring: Duncan Speirs, Kim Miettinen & Struan Tonnar all 1+0, Steven Moore, James Hutchinson, Connor Henderson & Joe Coulter all 0+1

Barons Scoring: Josh Bruce 1+1, Andrew Whitehouse 1+0, Joe Henry & Tomas Janak both 0+1

Match Officials: David Farren – Referee, Stuart Smith – Linesman, Samuel Campbell - Linesman

Saturday 8th April 2017 – Play Off Semi Final
Billingham Stars 7 - Blackburn Hawks 3
Period Scores: 0-1, 4-1, 3-1
Shots On Goal: Stars 41 – Hawks 41 (11-12, 15-18, 15-11)
Penalties In Minutes: Stars 33 – Hawks 20

Stars Scoring: Chris Sykes 2+2, Daniel Palmebjork 2+1, Michael Elder 2+0, Jack Watkins 1+2, Callum Davies & Thomas Keeley both 0+2, James Moss, Andy Finn & Ben Davison all 0+1

Hawks Scoring: Aaron Davies, Josef Istocky & Thomas Parkinson all 1+0, James Royds, Richard Bentham, James Riddoch, Steven Duncombe & Robert Streetly all 0+1

Match Officials: Haydn Hunter – Linesman, Roy Hamilton – Referee, David Emmerson - Linesman

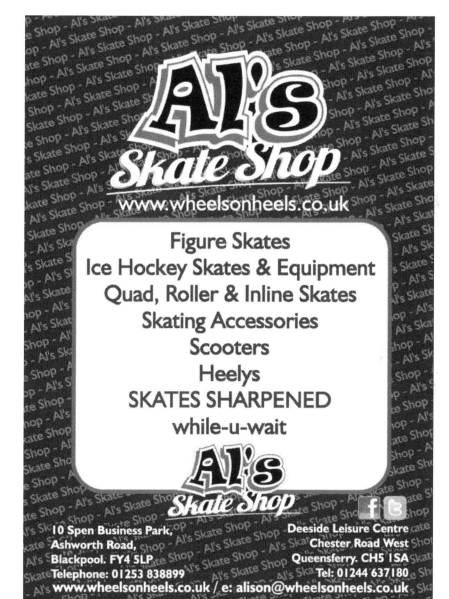

NIHL North - Laidler Conference

Laidler Conference champions Blackburn Eagles (Photo by Ella Thornton – Hawk Photography)

Top goalscorer and overall points scorer in the Laidler Conference was Richard Hagger of Hull Jets with 31+39 in 27 games. (Photo by Fiona Haggar)

Stuart Brittle of Widnes Wild notched up the most assists with 40 in 26 games (Photo by Geoff White – www.gw-images.com)

NIHL North - Laidler Conference

Final League Table – Laidler Conference 2016/17

Team	P	W	D	L	F	A	+/-	PIM	Pts
Blackburn Eagles	28	20	3	4	155	67	88	578	44
Widnes Wild	28	20	2	6	136	77	59	628	42
Altrincham Aces	28	16	3	9	125	97	28	834	35
Senators	28	14	6	8	133	95	38	800	34
Nottingham Lions	28	13	7	8	114	91	23	403	33
Hull Jets	28	9	3	16	105	145	-40	483	21
Bradford Bulldogs	28	4	1	23	99	181	-82	441	9
Coventry Blaze	28	2	1	24	51	165	-114	533	6

Note: Blackburn Eagles v Coventry Blaze not played - awarded as a 0-0 draw with 1 point each.
Hull Jets v Altrincham Aces awarded 0-5 win due to no ice available at Hull.

Leading Points Scorers 2016/17

Player	Team	GP	G	A	Pts	PIM
Richard Haggar	Hull Jets	27	31	39	70	22
Stuart Brittle	Widnes Wild	26	19	40	59	28
Kieran Beach	Hull Jets	26	27	29	56	34
Nathan Parkes-Britton	Sheffield Senators	28	26	28	54	4
Oliver Barron	Widnes Wild	28	30	22	52	24
Andrew Brown	Bradford Bulldogs	28	15	34	49	20
Nicholas Manning	Widnes Wild	23	14	30	44	20
Stefan Pristas	Bradford Bulldogs	27	28	15	43	12
Elliott Knell	Sheffield Senators	25	19	20	39	79
Brian Worrall	Altrincham Aces	24	13	26	39	8

Top Netminders – Laidler Conference 2016/17

Netminder	Team	GP	SA	GA	Sv%	SO
Matthew Milhench	Blackburn Eagles	10	34	1	97.06%	1
Nicholas Saxton	Blackburn Eagles	20	188	11	94.15%	1
Phil Crosby	Blackburn Eagles	24	761	55	92.77%	1
Mark Hartley	Sheffield Senators	15	478	36	92.47%	0
Declan Ryan	Altrincham Aces	21	732	58	92.08%	1
Greg Ruxton	Widnes Wild	21	302	24	92.05%	3
Thomas Hovell	Nottingham Lions	25	844	68	91.94%	2
Matthew Croyle	Widnes Wild	22	484	40	91.74%	3

*Blackburn Eagles team manager Darren Shaw and coaches Scott Barnett and Paul Burns with the league trophy.
(Photo by Ella Thornton – Hawk Photography).*

Laidler Conference Review

This season's Laidler Conference had the closest finish of any NIHL league competition for several years, with Blackburn Eagles eventually taking the title - just two points ahead of runners up Widnes Wild - and both teams finishing up with the same number of wins.

Three different teams topped the table over the course of the season and, while by Christmas it already looked as if the Eagles would probably end up on top of the pile, all of the top four played their part in making this a really exciting league season.

It was a season when everybody could beat everybody else and even the bottom half teams provided some very close games and took points off some of the higher placed sides at some point. Hull Jets' Richard Haggar finished up as the league's top scorer with 31+39 from 27 games and no one team dominated the scoring standings.

The early season talking point was the sudden departure of Widnes head coach Scott McKenzie who subsequently ended up at Deeside Dragons, taking several of last year's squad with him. Following the sad demise of Sheffield Spartans, their captain Ollie Barron was installed as the new player coach and he managed to entice several of his team mates to join him across the Pennines.

Sheffield Senators – relegated from the Moralee Conference after a nightmare winless season – also picked up a few Spartans and were a force to be reckoned with while Nottingham Lions – with their mix of youth and experience – were also expected to be there or thereabouts.

NIHL North - Laidler Conference

Games between Altrincham Aces and Widnes Wild were always feisty encounters.
(Photo by Geoff White - www.gw-images.com)

Altrincham Aces had a chequered season, taking points off the top teams on one hand and then losing to Bradford Bulldogs and Hull Jets on the other. Things clicked for them in the second half of the season, however, and they were able to mount a late charge for the play-offs.

But it was the Eagles who were the success story of this campaign. For many years, the team that finished bottom of the table every season – often without a win to show for all their efforts, this was a club that just kept on going.

Last season's fourth place finish was already acknowledged as a major achievement - but to go on and actually win the league was probably more than even the most partisan Blackburn fan could have expected.

The Eagles took over at the top of the league table after a 3-5 win away at Widnes in October and they stayed there for the rest of the season. But this was certainly no fluke as the Eagles had assembled their strongest ever team – with two overseas players for the first time in the shape of Tomas Mitrik - previously of Deeside Dragons - and Michal Fico who suddenly moved from Widnes days before the first meeting of the two teams.

There were no superstars in the Eagles team – no unstoppable "Palak"s in the line-up - and all the goals and assists throughout the season were shared around a number of players, with Chris Jones finishing the season as top scorer The team comprised a good mixture of former Blackburn Juniors, some acquisitions from elsewhere and a few ex-Hawks – notably last year's double winning captain Chris Arnone.

The subsequent announcement that the Eagles would be forced to fold at the end of the season overshadowed the Play Off weekend at iceSheffield. Widnes Wild shut out Altrincham Aces 2-0 in the first semi-final while a visibly under-par Eagles side lost out 1-3 to Sheffield Senators in the other.

The final went true to league form with the Wild overcoming the Senators 2-1 in a close and edgy encounter that saw the Widnes team pick up their first piece on silverware after 4 years of existence.

NIHL North - Laidler Conference

Altrincham Aces – Player Statistics 2016/17

Player	Regular Season					Laidler Play Offs				
	GP	G	A	Pts	PIM	GP	G	A	Pts	PIM
Brian Worrall	24	13	26	39	8	1	0	0	0	0
John Murray	23	15	21	36	58	1	0	0	0	2
Michael Gilbert	26	17	14	31	32	1	0	0	0	4
Jake Nurse	22	10	17	27	88	1	0	0	0	0
Jared Dickinson	18	8	15	23	55	1	0	0	0	2
Joe Greaves	18	17	6	23	165	0	0	0	0	0
Corey Lee	25	12	7	19	12	1	0	0	0	2
Tom Revesz	22	10	9	19	30	0	0	0	0	0
Andy Dunn	20	2	11	13	57	1	0	0	0	6
Daniel Berry	26	0	11	11	42	1	0	0	0	0
Steven Saunders	26	6	4	10	50	1	0	0	0	0
Pavel Slowik	10	2	8	10	54	1	0	0	0	0
Sheldon Cassidy	10	2	7	9	20	1	0	0	0	2
Cade Paul King	23	4	4	8	93	1	0	0	0	2
Thomas Gilbert	27	2	4	6	6	1	0	0	0	0
Declan Ryan	21	0	6	6	0	1	0	0	0	0
Luke Stretton	26	1	5	6	30	1	0	0	0	2
Jordan Holland	26	0	3	3	6	1	0	0	0	0
Marcin Laszczak	20	0	3	3	10	1	0	0	0	0
Sarah Hutchinson	19	0	2	2	2	0	0	0	0	0
Joel Cope	12	0	1	1	2	0	0	0	0	0
Scott Meakin	22	0	1	1	6	1	0	0	0	0
Levente Racz	2	0	1	1	0	0	0	0	0	0
Clara Janine Ashton	7	0	0	0	0	0	0	0	0	0
Samantha Bolwell	7	0	0	0	0	0	0	0	0	0
Adam Cherry	1	0	0	0	0	0	0	0	0	0
Jorge El-Hage	8	0	0	0	2	0	0	0	0	0
Aran Fox	13	0	0	0	4	0	0	0	0	0
Mason Howard	5	0	0	0	0	0	0	0	0	0
Philip Proudlove	3	0	0	0	0	0	0	0	0	0

Netminders	Regular Season					Laidler Play Offs			
	GP	SA	GA	Sv%	SO	GP	SA	GA	Sv%
Jorge El-Hage	8	156	7	95.51	1	0	0	0	0
Declan Ryan	21	732	58	92.08	1	1	27	2	92.59
Adam Cherry	1	33	3	90.91	0	0	0	0	0
Samantha Bolwell	7	83	8	90.36	0	0	0	0	0
Aran Fox	13	171	20	88.30	0	0	0	0	0

NIHL North - Laidler Conference

Altrincham Aces Team Photo by Paul Ferris

Standing (right to left): Robyn Crebbin (Head Coach), Rob Hutchinson (Joint Team Manager), Carol Holland, Tom Gilbert, Jared Dickinson, Dan Berry (A), Pavel Slovik, Jake Nurse (A), Joe Greaves, Andy Dunn, Tom Revesz, Mikey Gilbert, Luke Stretton, Scott Meakin, Corey Lee, Steve Saunders, John Murray Georgina Crebbin (Joint Manager), Liam Hesketh, Toni Gilbert, Rick Hesketh, Toni Gilbert, John Ardolino
Kneeling: Dave Holland, Elliott Bayne (Asst Coach), Jordan Holland, Marcin Laszczak, Brian Worrall ©. Front: netminders Declan Ryan & Samantha Bolwell
Missing from photo: Cade King, Joel Cope, Adam Cherry (nm), Jorge El Hage (nm), Aran Fox (nm), Sarah Hutchinson, CJ Linton (both on GB women's duty), Lily Greaves (Asst Coach), Stuart Latham (Media)

Blackburn Eagles Team Photo by Matt Strong
Back row: Harry Mercer, Steven Hetherington, Carl Slater, Chris Jones, Andrew Duxbury
Middle row: Darren Shaw, Kyle Haslam, Aaron Jordan, Jordan Ashington, Michal Fico, Richard Hughes, Tomas Mitrik, Craig Lutkevitch, Dave Williams, Daniel Fearon, Paul Burns, Bob Alexander
Front row: Nick Saxton, Chris Arnone, Wayne Slater, Phil Crosby, Sam Dunford, Scott Barnett, Matt Milhench

NIHL North - Laidler Conference

Blackburn Eagles – Player Statistics 2016/17

Player	Regular Season					Laidler Play Offs				
	GP	G	A	Pts	PIM	GP	G	A	Pts	PIM
Christopher Jones	25	21	17	38	48	1	0	0	0	12
Jordan Ashington	27	15	22	37	32	1	0	0	0	0
Aaron Jordan	26	21	15	36	46	1	0	0	0	2
Steven Hetherington	24	15	18	33	10	1	0	0	0	0
Michal Fico	22	6	25	31	28	1	0	0	0	0
Tomas Mitrik	25	17	14	31	61	1	0	1	1	0
Christopher Arnone	23	12	18	30	34	1	0	0	0	2
Wayne Slater	27	7	23	30	26	0	0	0	0	0
Sam Dunford	22	11	13	24	0	1	0	0	0	0
Craig Lutkevitch	27	3	17	20	84	1	1	0	1	0
Scott Barnett	24	12	5	17	43	1	0	0	0	0
Andrew Duxbury	26	6	8	14	8	1	0	0	0	0
Kyle Haslam	26	6	8	14	28	1	0	0	0	0
Carl Slater	27	2	8	10	72	1	0	0	0	4
David Williams	27	0	6	6	20	1	0	0	0	0
Richard Hughes	12	2	3	5	16	1	0	0	0	0
Daniel Fearon	18	0	3	3	2	1	0	0	0	0
Phil Crosby	24	0	2	2	2	1	0	0	0	10
Harry James Mercer	7	0	1	1	2	0	0	0	0	0
Callum Strong	3	0	1	1	0	0	0	0	0	0
Sean Jones	1	0	0	0	0	0	0	0	0	0
Matthew Milhench	10	0	0	0	0	0	0	0	0	0
Daniel Sanderson	1	0	0	0	0	0	0	0	0	0
Nicholas Saxton	20	0	0	0	0	1	0	0	0	0

Netminders	Regular Season					Laidler Play Offs			
	GP	SA	GA	Sv%	SO	GP	SA	GA	Sv%
Matt Milhench	10	34	1	97.06	1	0	0	0	0
Nicholas Saxton	20	188	11	94.15	1	0	0	0	0
Phil Crosby	24	761	55	92.77	1	1	31	3	90.32

The Eagles' trio of netminders, Matthew Milhench, Phil Crosby and Nick Saxton all topped the Laidler Conference netminder standings. (Photos l to r by Rob Hutchinson, John Milton and Matt Strong)

NIHL North - Laidler Conference

Bradford Bulldogs – Player Statistics 2016/17

Player	Regular Season				
	GP	G	A	Pts	PIM
Andrew Brown	28	15	34	49	20
Stefan Pristas	27	28	15	43	12
Dean Boothroyd	27	4	22	26	16
Myles David Dacres	19	10	15	25	22
Ben Spurgeon	27	3	10	13	31
Corey Stones	10	6	6	12	56
Alan Gray	14	8	3	11	6
Joshua James Richardson	24	5	6	11	6
Liam Salt	25	1	8	9	52
Mark Higson	24	4	4	8	18
Matthew Barlow	17	1	5	6	12
David Kamenicek	22	2	4	6	28
Mark Mcdonald	11	4	1	5	20
Macauley Stones	5	1	4	5	118
Michael Joseph Clancy	8	1	3	4	2
Willis Joel Nelson	24	1	3	4	8
Shannon Lingwood	5	2	1	3	2
Harry Palmer	6	2	1	3	2
Geraint Lewis	3	2	0	2	0
James Callum Royds	3	0	2	2	0
Alexander Marsden	8	0	1	1	4
Philip Pearson	15	0	1	1	2
Joshua Wiggins-Armitage	2	0	1	1	0
Ethan Jordi Armstrong	2	0	0	0	0
Jonah Armstrong	1	0	0	0	0
Jonathan Brown	1	0	0	0	0
Evan Coles	2	0	0	0	0
Michael Fletcher	2	0	0	0	0
Matthew Ian Fox	5	0	0	0	0
Hannah Victoria Gibson	1	0	0	0	0
Kristoffer Gibson	1	0	0	0	0
Warren James Gilfoyle	1	0	0	0	2
Ian Thirkettle	10	0	0	0	0
Russell Wackett	4	0	0	0	0

Bradford Bulldogs Netminders	Regular Season					
	GP	TOI	SA	GA	Sv%	SO
Warren James Gilfoyle	1	0	44	4	90.91%	0
Ian Thirkettle	10	7	380	37	90.26%	0
Philip Pearson	15	40	640	65	89.84%	1
Jonah Armstrong	1	56	61	8	86.89%	0
Ethan Jordi Armstrong	2	59	136	20	85.29%	0
Evan Coles	2	49	49	9	81.63%	0
Matthew Ian Fox	5	10	94	18	80.85%	0
Jonathan Brown	1	0	46	9	80.43%	0
Joshua Wiggins-Armitage	2	0	50	11	78.00%	0

NIHL North - Laidler Conference

Coventry Blaze – Player Statistics 2016/17

Player	Regular Season				
	GP	G	A	Pts	PIM
Brandon Anderton	18	6	8	14	36
Sam Tyler Prosser	24	5	9	14	86
Arthur Steven Brookes	23	8	4	12	6
Christoper Blackett	20	3	8	11	10
Sam Chandler	23	6	4	10	0
Luke Curtis	24	8	2	10	14
Stephen Crowe	25	2	4	6	22
Jordan Liddell	16	1	5	6	4
Adam Matteri	26	4	1	5	40
Anthony Pountney	24	0	5	5	16
Jordan Bloom	5	3	1	4	0
Jake Larkin	6	2	2	4	2
Jake Small	23	0	4	4	6
Dale Buckland	12	1	2	3	53
Connor Keyes	25	1	2	3	70
Jack Connor Mckay	9	0	3	3	0
Scott Venus	23	0	3	3	73
Zac Chamberlain	22	0	2	2	63
Josh Mannion	23	1	0	1	2
Connor McNaughton	5	0	1	1	0
Daniel Thomason	19	0	1	1	8
Daniel Thomas Burton	1	0	0	0	12
Joshua Crane	5	0	0	0	0
Graham James Laverick	21	0	0	0	0
James Lindley	13	0	0	0	0
David Roxburgh	27	0	0	0	0
Lewis James Smith	2	0	0	0	2
Mariah Spare	1	0	0	0	0

Coventry Blaze Netminders	Regular Season					
	GP	TOI	SA	GA	Sv%	SO
Joshua Crane	5	0	60	6	90.00%	0
Graham James Laverick	21	32	608	68	88.82%	0
David Roxburgh	27	9	713	91	87.24%	0

NIHL North - Laidler Conference

Hull Jets – Player Statistics 2016/17

Player	Regular Season				
	GP	G	A	Pts	PIM
Richard Haggar	27	31	39	70	22
Kieran Beach	26	27	29	56	34
Jay Robinson	24	16	16	32	60
Jamie Lewis	27	1	15	16	48
Joshua James Blissett	14	10	5	15	54
Thomas Andrew Forster	27	7	5	12	18
Corey Stones	3	6	6	12	56
Daniel Spence	21	1	5	6	38
Harry Bridges	19	1	3	4	8
Alex Foreman	26	0	4	4	22
Bryn Byron Gooch	15	2	2	4	18
James Patrick Robinson	5	3	1	4	2
Brady Doxey	7	1	2	3	4
Cameron King	13	1	1	2	10
Callum Rawson	2	0	2	2	0
Kieran Robinson	6	0	2	2	0
Raivis Sadinovs	16	1	1	2	61
Adam Simpson	11	0	2	2	2
Samuel Warnock	22	0	2	2	10
Joseph Anson	17	0	1	1	14
Cameron Ross Glasby	4	0	1	1	2
Braden Jennings	3	0	1	1	0
James Maughan	5	0	1	1	2
Elliot Meadows	1	1	0	1	0
Joel Simon Newlove	15	1	0	1	2
Thomas Robjohns	5	0	1	1	0
Dean Andrew Bowater	26	0	0	0	4
David Good	5	0	0	0	0
Steven Graham Hudson	1	0	0	0	0
Oliver Mitchell	1	0	0	0	0
Mairis Sadinovs	17	0	0	0	34

Netminder	Regular Season					
	GP	TOI	SA	GA	Sv%	SO
Steven Graham Hudson	1	0	46	5	89.13%	0
Dean Andrew Bowater	26	18	1061	128	87.94%	1
David Good	5	40	45	6	86.67%	0

NIHL North - Laidler Conference

Hull Jets Team Photo by Arthur Foster

Nottingham Lions Team Photo
Standing (left to right): (Adam Andrews, Robert Perks, Ben Wilson, Jordan Wright, Joe Gretton, Luke smith, Elliott Perrin, Joe Humphries, Ondrej Piniok, Sam Jackson, Paul Glossop (Coach), Cam Pyewell, Paul Stanley, Matt Bradbury (Coach).
Kneeling (left to right): Luke Thomas, Tom Hovell (Netminder), Daniel Hazeldine, Daniel Harrison (Team GM), Jamie Hovell, Ben Wood

NIHL North - Laidler Conference

Nottingham Lions – Player Statistics 2016/17

Player	Regular Season				
	GP	G	A	Pts	PIM
Ondrej Pniok	23	18	18	36	6
Paul Stanley	28	17	16	33	26
Daniel James Hazeldine	23	20	10	30	47
Joe Humphries	22	8	15	23	20
Adam Andrews	27	5	17	22	26
Ben Wood	26	11	10	21	32
Elliot Perrin	26	4	12	16	28
Cameron Pywell	24	8	7	15	10
Luke Thomas	26	1	9	10	12
Jamie Hovell	23	2	7	9	6
Joseph James Gretton	25	5	3	8	32
Stuart Parker	7	3	4	7	2
Robert Perks	28	4	3	7	70
Liam Redwood	19	3	4	7	10
Luke Smith	28	3	4	7	40
Samuel Jackson	23	0	4	4	0
Benjamin Wilson	27	2	2	4	26
Harry Hopkins	10	0	2	2	2
Steven Bicker	9	0	1	1	0
Stephen Gilmartin	2	0	1	1	0
Connor Hardy	13	0	1	1	0
Joseph Noel Hazeldine	1	0	1	1	0
Thomas Hovell	25	0	1	1	2
Angus Laing	2	0	1	1	0
Jack Matthew Crowston	1	0	0	0	0
Myles Dallison	9	0	0	0	0
Zachary Glossop	9	0	0	0	0
Richard Gray	2	0	0	0	0
Alan Levers	2	0	0	0	0
Declan Orange	2	0	0	0	0
Archie Payne	1	0	0	0	0
Jordan Wright	25	0	0	0	0

Netminder	Regular Season					
	GP	TOI	SA	GA	Sv%	SO
Angus Laing	2	9	100	5	95.00%	2
Thomas Hovell	25	17	844	68	91.94%	2
Myles Dallison	9	18	47	4	91.49%	1
Steven Bicker	9	0	36	4	88.89%	0
Alan Levers	2	40	72	9	87.50%	0
Stephen Gilmartin	2	20	7	2	71.43%	0

NIHL North - Laidler Conference

Sheffield Senators – Player Statistics 2016/17

Player	Regular Season					Laidler Play Offs				
	GP	G	A	Pts	PIM	GP	G	A	Pts	PIM
Nathan Parkes-Britton	28	26	28	54	4	2	1	0	1	2
Elliott Knell	25	19	20	39	79	2	1	0	0	2
Thomas Proctor	21	14	17	31	4	2	1	1	2	0
Alexander Harding	23	13	17	30	72	2	0	1	1	0
Thomas Humphries	22	12	18	30	26	0	0	0	0	0
George Crawshaw	24	8	13	21	10	2	1	0	1	0
Shaun Wild	23	6	13	19	26	2	0	0	0	0
Stephen Weeks	26	3	12	15	58	2	0	0	0	2
Arran Bell	26	5	9	14	42	0	0	0	0	0
Cameron Brownley	4	7	4	11	82	0	0	0	0	0
Ryan Colston Fraley	17	2	6	8	10	2	0	0	0	0
Paul Lofthouse	24	1	7	8	108	2	0	0	0	6
Andrew McEwan	15	2	6	8	32	1	0	0	0	0
Jonathan Bell	14	0	5	5	14	2	0	0	0	2
Joe Timothy Cross	13	2	2	4	12	2	0	0	0	4
Lewis George Jones	25	3	0	3	40	2	0	0	0	0
Jordon Lee Martin	27	1	2	3	24	2	0	0	0	0
Lewis Jon Otley	12	1	2	3	10	2	0	0	0	0
Sam John Rodgers	11	1	2	3	0	2	0	0	0	0
Jamie Scott	13	2	1	3	6	0	0	0	0	0
Matthew Wain	11	1	1	2	92	1	0	0	0	0
Jack Henry Brain	10	1	0	1	0	2	0	1	1	0
Arron Hudson	8	0	1	1	0	1	0	0	0	0
Sam Hurst	2	1	0	1	2	0	0	0	0	0
Angus Laing	5	0	1	1	0	0	0	0	0	0
Jamie Pyewell	17	1	0	1	8	2	0	0	0	2
John-Henry Walker	11	1	0	1	25	2	0	0	0	0
Thomas Barkworth	4	0	0	0	0	0	0	0	0	0
Robert Browne	25	0	0	0	0	2	0	0	0	0
Evan Coles	1	0	0	0	0	0	0	0	0	0
Jack John Edgar	1	0	0	0	0	0	0	0	0	0
Joseph Gent	1	0	0	0	0	0	0	0	0	0
Mark Hartley	15	0	0	0	6	2	0	0	0	0

Netminder	Regular Season						Laidler Play Offs				
	GP	TOI	SA	GA	Sv%	SO	GP	TOI	SA	GA	Sv%
Angus Laing	5	9	100	5	95.00	2	0	0	0	0	0
Mark Hartley	15	59	478	36	92.47	0	2	119.55	86	3	96.51
Robert Browne	25	10	529	53	89.98	2	0	0	0	0	0
Thomas Barkworth	4	0	36	4	88.89	0	0	0	0	0	0
Evan Coles	1	49	49	9	81.63	0	0	0	0	0	0
Empty Net	0	0	0	0	0	0	1	00.05	0	0	0

NIHL North - Laidler Conference

Sheffield Senators Team Photo by CLM Photography

Back Row (l to r): Barbara Walker (Manager), John-Henry Walker, George Crawshaw, Arron Hudson, Matt Darlow, Lewis Jones, Alex Harding, Paul Lofthouse, Ryan Fraley, George Cross, Lewis Otley, Matt Wain, Jack Brain, Sam Rodgers, Luke Martin
Middle Row: Angus Laing, Jonny Bell, Jordon Martin, Nathan Britton, Andrew Chapman (Hd Coach), Arran Bell, Olly Knell (Coach), Jamie Pyewell, Elliott Knell.   Front Row: 2 netminders Mark Hartley & Bobby Browne.

Widnes Wild Team Photo by Geoff White – www.gw-images.com

Back Row (left to right): Jon Anderson (Team Manager), Martina Bencova (Physio), Danny Bullock, Kieran Strangeway, Nick Manning, Tom Ratcliffe, Mike Mawer, Andrew Turner, Lee Kemp, Tom Jackson, Berwyn Hughes, Ken Armstrong, Will Barron, Chris Preston, Mark Gillingham (Asst Coach), Callum Fraine (Asst Coach).   Front Row (left to right): Greg Ruxton, Pavel Vales, Stuart Brittle, Shaun Dippnall, Matt Croyle, Ollie Barron (Head Coach), David Swanston, Joe Gilbert, Tom McDonald

NIHL North - Laidler Conference

Widnes Wild Player Statistics - Season 2016/17

Player	Laidler Conference					Promotion			Play Offs		
	GP	G	A	Pts	PIM	GP	Pts	PIM	GP	Pts	PIM
Stuart Brittle	26	19	40	59	28	1	0	6	2	2	16
Oliver Barron	28	30	22	52	24	1	1	2	2	3	2
Nicholas Manning	23	14	30	44	20	1	2	2	2	3	2
Shaun Dippnall	24	8	19	27	28	1	1	0	2	1	2
Pavel Vales	24	4	20	24	18	1	1	0	2	0	0
Will Barron	16	10	10	20	6	1	0	0	2	0	0
Daniel Bullock	22	10	5	15	26	1	0	0	2	0	0
Karl Niamatali	14	6	9	15	8	0	0	0	2	0	2
Andrew Turner	24	4	11	15	76	1	0	12	2	1	0
Simon Offord	15	3	11	14	22	1	0	2	2	1	0
Berwyn Hughes	27	5	8	13	52	1	1	0	2	1	12
Bobby Caunce	9	6	5	11	2	1	1	25	0	0	0
Sheldon Cassidy	8	2	7	9	20	0	0	0	0	0	0
Kieran Strangeway	25	3	6	9	58	1	1	0	2	0	0
Joseph Gilbert	18	1	7	8	16	0	0	0	0	0	0
Lee Kemp	26	1	6	7	74	1	0	0	2	0	4
Ken Armstrong	26	3	3	6	12	1	0	0	2	0	0
Michael Mawer	24	1	4	5	26	1	0	10	2	0	0
Thomas Ratcliffe	19	4	1	5	100	1	0	0	2	0	2
Thomas Jackson	25	1	3	4	12	1	0	2	2	0	0
David Swanston	22	2	1	3	4	0	0	0	2	0	0
Michal Fico	2	1	1	2	0	0	0	0	0	0	0
Thomas McDonald	6	0	1	1	0	0	0	0	2	0	0
Christopher Preston	16	0	1	1	6	0	0	0	2	0	0
Matthew Croyle	22	0	0	0	2	1	0	0	2	0	0
Greg Ruxton	21	0	0	0	0	0	0	0	2	0	0

Widnes Wild Netminder Statistics - Season 2016/17

Laidler Conference	GP	SA	GA	SA%	S/O
Greg Ruxton	21	302	24	92.05%	3
Thomas McDonald	6	136	11	91.91%	1
Matthew Croyle	22	484	40	91.74%	3

Matt Croyle – Total Netminder Statistics 2016/17

	GP	Shots	GA	SA%	S/O
Laidler Conference	22	484	40	91.74%	3
Promotion Game	1	45	4	91.11%	0
Play Offs	2	55	1	98.00%	1
Totals	25	584	45	92.29%	4

NIHL North - Laidler Conference

Photos from top: Widnes Wild celebrate their Play Off trophy, Goal action from the Play Off Final, Widnes Wild Captain Shaun Dippnall receives the trophy (Photos by John Milton).Sheffield Senators celebrate their semi-final win (Keith and Jenny Davies). Altrincham Aces and Blackburn Eagles after their semi- final defeats (Matthew Donnachie, Pyro Media).

NIHL North - Laidler Conference

Sunday 9th April 2017 – Play Off Final
Widnes Wild 2 – Sheffield Senators 1 (at iceSheffield)
Period Scores: 1-0, 1-0, 0-1
Shots On Goal: Widnes 45 – Sheffield 23 (18-11, 11-8, 16-4)
Penalties In Minutes: Widnes 8 – Sheffield 8

Widnes Scoring: Shaun Dippnall 1+0, Ollie Barron 1+0, Andrew Turner, Nick Manning, Berwyn Hughes, Stuart Brittle all 0+1

Senators Scoring: Elliott Knell 1+0

Widnes Players: *Andrew Turner, Karl Niamatali, Will Barron, Oliver Barron, Ken Armstrong – A, Daniel Bullock, David Swanston, Lee Kemp, Nicholas Manning, Berwyn Hughes, Simon Offord, Stuart Brittle – A, Pavel Vales, Thomas McDonald, Matthew Croyle – NM, Thomas Ratcliffe, Christopher Preston, Kieran Strangeway, Greg Ruxton – NM, Thomas Jackson, Michael Mawer, Shaun Dippnall - C*

Sheffield Players: *Jack Henry Brain, Jonathan Bell, Arron Hudson, George Crawshaw, John-Henry Walker, Joe Timothy Cross, Thomas Proctor, Lewis Jon Otley, Stephen Weeks, Elliott Knell – A, Nathan Parkes-Britton – C, Sam John Rodgers, Jordon Lee Martin, Paul Lofthouse – A, Alexander Harding, Robert Browne – NM, Mark Hartley – NM, Lewis George Jones, Ryan Colston Fraley, Jamie Pyewell, Shaun Wild*

Match Officials: Oliver Truswell – Linesman, Juris Susters – Referee, Robert James Pullar – Linesman

Saturday 8th April 2017 – Play Off Semi Final
Widnes Wild 2 – Altrincham Aces 0 (at iceSheffield)
Period Scores: 0-0, 1-0, 1-0
Shots On Goal: Widnes 27 – Aces 32 (8-8, 10-13, 9-11)
Penalties In Minutes: Widnes 36 – Aces 24

Widnes Scoring: Ollie Barron 2+0, Nick Manning 0+2, Simon Offord & Stuart Brittle 0+1
Netminder Matt Croyle: 32-shot shut out.

Match Officials: Robert James Pullar – Linesman, Mitchell Kempster – Referee, Joseph Baggaley -Linesman

Saturday 8th April 2017 – Play Off Semi Final
Blackburn Eagles 1 – Sheffield Senators 3
Period Scores: 0-3, 1-0, 0-0
Shots On Goal: Eagles – Senators 31 (13-14, 14-8, 14-9)
Penalties In Minutes: Eagles 30 – Senators 12

Eagles Scoring: Craig Lutkevich 1+0, Tomas Mitrik 0+1
Senators Scoring: Thomas Proctor 1+1, George Crawshaw & Nathan Parkes-Britton 1+0, Alex Harding 0+1

Match Officials: Oliver Truswell – Linesman, Juris Susters – Referee, Adam David Hands – Linesman

NIHL North – Promotion Game

James Parsons celebrates the Dragons' OT winning goal (photo by Peter Sheffield – www.psd-images.com)

Sunday 2nd April 2017 – Promotion Game
Dragons (Deeside) 4 - Widnes Wild 3   (at Blackburn Arena)
Period Scores: 1-1, 2-2, 0-0, 1-0
Shots on Goal: Dragons 45 – Widnes 33   (12-12, 11-12, 15-6, 7-3)
Penalties In Minutes: Dragons 53 – Widnes 61

Dragons Scoring: Jordan Bannon 2+0, Filip Supa 1+1, James Parsons 1+0, Joseph Hazeldine and Scott McKenzie 0+2, Geoff Wigglesworth & Matthew Wainwright 0+1.

Widnes Scoring: Nick Manning 1+1, Bobby Caunce & Berwyn Hughes both 1+0, Ollie Barron, Pavel Vales, Kieran Strangeway & Pavel Vales all 0+1
Match Officials: Haydn Hunter – Linesman, David Emmerson – Referee, Samuel Campbell - Linesman

The NIHL North promotion game was a close run thing this year – following on from Widnes Wild's two previous appearances in the same tie which had ended up in a 5-0 shut-out by Sheffield Spartans last year and a two legged 20-5 defeat by the Whitley Warriors the season before.

Opponents Deeside Dragons had staged a bit of a relegation "great escape" by pulling themselves off the bottom of the Moralee table and into the play-off game in their very last game of the season the night before and were up for the challenge,

In a fascinating, close matched game, the Dragons took the lead three times but were pegged back each time by the Wild and, with the score 3-3 after 60 minutes, the game went into sudden death 4 on 4 overtime.

Both teams had chances in the extra phase but, just as it looked as if the game were heading for a penalty shootout, the Dragons fired in a dramatic winner with just 51 seconds on the clock to maintain their place in the Moralee season for another season.

NIHL North

Fylde Coast Ice Arena - August 2014 to April 2017

Exterior of Fylde Coast Ice Arena – August 2016 (Photo by Paul Breeze)

September / October 2014 - Blackpool Seagulls U16 games at FCIA. No seating is installed and spectator accommodating is restricted to standing behind the benches. The right hand photo is particularly interesting as it shows how the wall prevents spectators getting along the full length of the ice. The team benches are on either side of the half way line but the scorers' bench is right at the far end.

(Photo left by Paul Breeze / Photo right by Marina Frankel)

The newly installed balcony seating at a Manchester Phoenix EPL match at Fylde Coast Ice Arena, September 2016. Note that the offending wall is still in place to the right of picture. (FCIA Facebook Page)

Blackpool Seagulls rec team at FCIA in 2017

Following on from the cruel closure of the Isle of Wight Arena back in October, British ice hockey lost another of its precious venues in May 2017 when the Fylde Coast Ice Arena in Blackpool suddenly closed permanently.

While Blackpool has a proud ice hockey history stretching back to the late 1930s (see following page), the FCIA venue itself had a rather short and chequered existence – the full story of which we will save for another time.

It had opened in August 2014 and boasted a full size (56mx26m) ice pad and even a second smaller "performance "ice pad as well. Unfortunately, the building was opened without any seating for spectators and that made it unsuitable for running a competitive ice hockey team without any revenue from home games.

Several recreational teams used the venue for training and informal scrimmages and a few Blackpool Seagulls Under 16 league games were played there in the 2014/15 season and but it was the shock announcement that Manchester Phoenix would play their EPL games there for the 2016/17 season that finally put FCIA on the map.

A few seats were hurriedly installed on the balcony but the approx. 200 capacity was never going to be enough for EPL crowds and the venue attracted a lot of criticism from Phoenix and visiting fans alike. The Manchester team ran out of money in January and played a couple more home games at Widnes before folding completely.

There were still vague hopes that the FCIA could support junior hockey and an NIHL 2 but these were dealt a blow when the venue closed temporarily in April to carry out maintenance on its chilling plant.

Worse news was to follow on 21st May when the FCIA management made the following announcement on their Facebook page:

"As many of you are aware, we have experienced a major problem with our refrigeration plant. The management have worked very hard to resolve the issue but it appears the equipment needed to make the ice is beyond repair. The logistical and technical challenges that this site presents, particularly the reliance upon external diesel power generation, have taken their toll on our chiller plant. As replacement equipment would be subject to the same conditions we have been advised that it is not viable to continue operating from this location.

We have instructed contractors to dismantle and remove the rinks and as a result the Arena on Bristol Avenue will be closed permanently."

Blackpool Ice Hockey Timeline 1937 to 2017

Dec 1937: Pleasure Beach "Ice Drome" opens - exhibition games are staged

1951: Blackpool Seagulls team formed – win Midland Intermediate league. Ice hockey is played continuously at Blackpool throughout the 1950, 60, 70s and 80s. (For more details about Blackpool Seagulls during this period see "The Seagull Has Landed" - ISBN 9781909643017)

1992: Ice hockey ceases at Ice Drome, all teams move to Blackburn

April 2011: Subzero Arena opens in Cleveleys, Wyre Seagulls team formed.

July 2011: Fylde Flyers league team announced

10th December 2011: First Fylde Flyers home game

17th December 2012: Wyre Seagulls v Blackpool Raiders – Raiders subsequently reform as Seagulls rec team

25th February 2012: Blackpool Seagulls play UK Firefighters team in front of SubZero record crowd.

March 2013: Fylde Flyers fold after just two seasons. Wyre and Blackpool teams continue to play rec hockey.

Summer 2013: Cleveleys rink changes owners – no upkeep work is done and facility begins to suffer.

August 2014: Full sized Fylde Coast Ice Arena opens in Bispham, Blackpool

28th September 2014: Blackpool Seagulls junior team play Deeside Dragons in EIHA Under 16 league in the first ever competitive game in Blackpool for over 20 years and first ever on a full size ice surface. Cleveleys Arena closes the same day, citing unfair competition.

February 2015: Cleveleys rink reopens as a "community interest" concern. FCIA management react by barring anybody who might have anything to do with the "new" rink and trying to impose unfair terms on junior hockey training sessions. Wyre Seagulls, Seagulls juniors and some rec players move back to Cleveleys. FCIA announce own separate junior set-up and new rec teams.

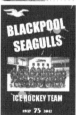

Feb / March 2015: Seagulls juniors are forced to play under 16 "home" games at Deeside and Widnes as Cleveleys rink is no longer on EIHA list of venues.

October 2015: Cleveleys rink closes for refurbishment and never reopens again. Building eventually becomes an indoor trampoline /play centre. Wyre Seagulls switch to Blackburn.

Season 2015/16: FCIA team enters EIHA North junior leagues and gets hammered in every game.

August 2016: Surprise announcement that Manchester Phoenix will play their EPL home games at FCIA. 17 games are played in total (4 wins) before Phoenix move briefly to Widnes in January.

27th November 2016: Blackpool Seagulls lose 0-1 to Streatham Night Wolves in rec challenge game

7th January 2017: Last competitive game played at FCIA is Phoenix EPL 1-7 defeat to Guildford Flames

22nd April 2017: Seagulls Vets v North West All Stars charity game has to be cancelled due to technical problems with FCIA rink.

21st May 2017: Announcement that FCIA has closed permanently.

Interview with Dave Carr - by Chris Randall, NIHL South Editor

Dave Carr's last game for Streatham (Photos by Rick Webb Photographic)

Interview with Dave Carr - by Chris Randall, NIHL South Editor

Born in Durham in the North East, with that thick Geordie accent, what age did you first step foot on the ice and what rink would it have been?

I first skated at Durham at around the age of 8 I think and I started playing hockey when I was 10. My cousins both played and we started to watch some games at both junior level and of course the Wasps and really got into it. At the time Durham were British Champions at most levels so when you went to training as a beginner there was no guarantee you would make the team. I hated it to be honest when I first started. I had second hand kit and it didn't always fit properly, plus the training was hard and if you couldn't do things very well it was really embarrassing as the coaching was old school. It took me a couple of years to actually enjoy playing the game so I thank my parents for making me stick at it. When I think back to my Mam picking up my brother and I from school, we used to get changed in the car on the way to the rink for training and walk out of it in our full kit and skate guards on. It wouldn't have been so bad if it hadn't have been a tiny Ford Fiesta!

What are your fondest memories growing up playing through Juniors?

Most of it was brilliant. Travelling to tournaments in Fife and Cardiff, going abroad to Czech and Canada all shape your life at an early age. When I was younger there were less teams around so while my mates were sitting at home playing on the Sega Mega Drive, I was heading off on a team bus to Solihull, Trafford or Peterborough to play hockey. It opened my eyes to the rest of the UK and I met so many good people. That's the real positive of playing in a minority sport where you have to travel to play.

The mighty Durham Wasps were a Dynasty in the Eighties and early Nineties, was the rink as bad as for the opponents as they made out, with stories of cold shower, and dire facilities for the visitors? What are your memories of the place, packed with 4,000 fans?

The rink was a dump but if you fill any building with passionate people and of course a winning team then it becomes a special place. You can see that at old music venues like Brixton Academy too. I remember sitting on a pipe at the back of the stand behind the goal because you couldn't get a seat and the atmosphere was electric. I remember the Jean Michel-Jarre music they played, the damp smell of the place and that classic scoreboard. The showers were cold and the windows were almost always smashed so a wind would whip in from the river while you were getting changed. In fairness most rinks were pretty bad back then and even now, most still haven't managed to plumb in decent warm showers and its 2017! The opposition would moan about bad facilities but in fairness we used to train with cones on the ice half the time, but not for drill purposes, just to stop you skating over the patches of concrete. I remember the first game I watched at Sheffield Arena when the Steelers arrived to change UK hockey forever, and that was also great in its own way, but give me a packed rink over an Arena any day of the week for atmosphere. I feel sorry for those people who missed watching the hockey in the Heineken days. The standard wasn't the greatest but the atmosphere and entertainment was far better than now.

Of all the standout players that you have either watched or played with/ against who is your top 2 or 3 and what qualities did they possess?

That's a tough question. I have always played in the second or third tier so the standout players to me have always been those who lead by example and play the game in the right way. I look at former captains like Oxford's Darron Elliott and Streatham's Joe Johnston for example. Two players who genuinely love their respective clubs and would play every game they could at 100%. It's easy to keep going when things are going well or when you are getting a decent wedge of cash for your troubles, but quality players playing for the right reasons will always get my respect.

Which teams had the biggest rivalry against the Wasps?

Whitley of course. It went right through to the juniors and in truth, Whitley didn't like anyone to be fair. I also played for Sunderland and Billingham and games up at Hillheads were always feisty affairs. One of my last ever games up North was for Billingham at Whitley and we had to be locked in the changing room afterwards for our own safety. The crowd were going crazy and there were chairs being hurled around the penalty box and players were fighting in the corridors under the stands. It was absolutely nuts but we won and knocked them out of the play-offs so it was a good

Interview with Dave Carr - by Chris Randall, NIHL South Editor

memory overall. Its a disgrace the North East lost Durham and Sunderland rinks and it would be great if they could build another facility on Wearside.

You moved down South many years ago playing against myself at one point having a season or two of rec hockey . What circumstances made you drop down from League hockey , and how did it differ from League Hockey?

I signed for Haringey Greyhounds in the old EPL and we had a really bad season. They'd accepted promotion after doing reasonably well in ED1 but the team was nowhere near good enough despite having a few decent players. The atmosphere in the locker room was toxic thanks to a clash of personalities and it really wasn't a nice experience at all. When I later became a senior player at other clubs I always tried to make sure that I contributed to making it a nice place to play. The changing room should be a place you feel welcome and enjoy yourself. In many cases in later seasons the time spent with the lads in the room was actually more fun than being on the ice.

Anyway, I lived near Alexandra Palace so I started skating with a few recreational teams at least 3 or 4 times a week. The people who play rec pay out of their own money for the pleasure, are there because they want to be there and most have an appetite to get better – it was such a positive experience with good people. When the new season started and Haringey were starting another season I just thought why bother. I didn't have a car to travel and play elsewhere (there were no senior teams in London anyway at the time), I had decent job on the Underground and had no desire to waste my weekends in such an environment.

Playing in Haringey and Oxford and later in your career Streatham, was there one highlight or person from any of those organisations you still keep in touch with? Do you find yourself still routing for them at all?

All of my time at Oxford was a highlight, I absolutely loved it from the minute I walked through the door. I bawled my eyes out when I left which was a little embarrassing, but I could never have guessed how much Streatham and the players I would ice with would get under my skin over the following 7 years. It was such an honour to be around at such an important time in the clubs history. Escaping relegation at Slough on the last day of the season, getting man of the match in the last ever game at the old Streatham Arena and then playing the first game in the new rink. It was amazing and helped me through tough times in my personal life too. I would love to see someone make a success of hockey at the Palace, I had four spells at Haringey and played poorly each time, but that's not to say I didn't make a lot of friends up there.

Well known for your Prohockeynews work, how much time does that take out of your weekend and how do you feel with the new changes to the League heading forward into the new season?

It takes a lot of work and I am not going to lie, my enthusiasm has dampened a lot after the events of this summer. I noticed Stewart Roberts announced he was hanging up the pen on his Ice Hockey Annual as he couldn't motivate himself anymore and that did strike a chord with me. The sport gets away with bad behaviour and organisation because in truth there is no media scrutiny and no one really cares outside of the hockey bubble and The Hockey Forum. I write because I want to promote the game and show the positive side so with the current league set up that makes it hard, especially when you know deep down it's flawed from Elite league down. I will keep writing for as long as I enjoy it but sometimes things just come to a natural end and the jokes wear thin.

Finally, Dave, with your brother Adam Carr signed for Streatham this coming season, will you watch him lighting it up for the Redhawks this year ?

I will go down and watch of course. I really hope he enjoys it and that the team do better than expected. In many ways if the league format hadn't changed Streatham would be looking at a title winning roster this year and instead they are aiming for mid table at best. The fans there were absolutely brilliant to me and it would be great if Adam and the boys can help give them something to shout about again this season.

Top photo: Aidan Doughty as a Wightlink Raider in season 2012/13 (Photo by Isle Of Wight County Press)
Above left: playing for the Superior Rough Riders in the Western States Hockey League (Photo by Mark Mauno)
Above Right: Playing for Solent Devils in the 2016/17 season. (Photo by Dave Chapman)

AIDAN DOUGHTY *Feature by Chris Randall*

It's often been said that there is a great amount of potential out there in young British players. The Annual Inter-Conference tournament that takes place in Hull is evidence of that. Plenty of aspiring Brits often take their talent overseas to try and progress in the sport, hoping that they can be in the shop window for some potential scouts, looking for their big break. NIHL South Editor Chris (Badger) Randall has seen one such youngster rise through the junior ranks on the Isle of Wight and make a seamless transition into Senior Hockey.

Born in 1995, dad Geoff Doughty had his son Aidan Doughty soon skating and playing within the Junior setup on the Isle of Wight. Holding the accolade of being one of the longest ever serving juniors from when he started to his last days as a member of the Wightlink Junior Raiders Under 18's side, he set scoring records that made people realise that this kid has bags of talent and potential.

Looking back on that Junior career, his stats were incredible. In 54 Under 16's matches he scored 144 goals and 40 assists for 184 points. Then in 48 games at Under 18s level, another mind boggling 147 goals and 45 assists for 192 points was just as impressive.

Most people who know Aidan knew he could score, he was never overly physical but highly skilled and has a calmness about him on the ice that belied his early years.

He stepped into senior hockey whilst splitting time with the Juniors. Wightlink Tigers was his first foray into senior hockey playing 15 games with 7 goals and 9 assists. Not too bad to kick start his NIHL Division 2 career off with.

Wightlink Raiders Head Coach Jeremy Cornish soon had him in the lineup for 10 games in the 2011/2012 season. The following season - 2012/2013 - Aidan featured in 21 games for the Wightlink Raiders whilst appearing in 5 Division 2 games with the Tigers.

A move to the States came about in 2012/2013 for young Doughty as he tried his luck in the WSHL. The Boulder Jr Bison was where he skated in 21 contests returning 4 goals and 5 assists.

Speaking with Aidan over the summer back then (2013) he spoke of the difference in the standard and how the game was over there. Rolling 4 lines, 35-45 second shifts and most his age being 6'2 and 190 pounds or more it was a physical game and faster. It was good to test himself and see how he measured himself up n this good junior league.

Enjoying it so much, he decided to play the 2013/2014 season with a new challenge and new chapter as he suited up in 37 games still in the WSHL with the Colorado Rough Riders, upping his points total with 12 goals and 25 points from 37 outings.

Into the 2014/2015 season, his third consecutive year in the WSHL, the Superior Rough Riders was where he bagged 18 goals and 23 assists in 52 games. Always low penalty minutes exemplified Aidan's quality as a strong player with good discipline. He brought some physicality into his game after honing it for 3 years in the States and building some size to his 6'2 frame.

NIHL South

2016/2017 saw the former Island Junior return to his home town club the Wightlink Raiders as Head Coach Jeremy Cornish was only too happy to secure him for the season.

Unfortunately, Aiden suddenly found himself club less when the Isle of Wight rink that the Wightlink Raiders played out of was repossessed by the buildings landlords in a dispute.

It wasn't long on the sidelines however, as Solent Devils Player-Coach Alex Murray enticed him to conclude the season at the South Coast club. Good for 37 points, 17 goals and 20 assists, he was a threat every time he stepped on the ice. Winning a host of awards at season's end, the low budget Club the Solent Devils were always going to have a battle to re-sign the talented 6'2 180 pound forward.

2017/2018 will see Doughty re-united with his former Wightlink Raiders, now Streatham Redhawks Coach, Jeremy Cornish in the Capital this coming season where the bar has been raised with the additions of the former EPL clubs.

No doubt defences will be stretched to the limit when the skilled centre man takes to the ice come September.

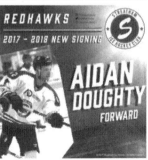

Above: with the Boulder Junior Bison in 2013/14
Top right: as a 15 year old junior at Wightlink
(Photo by Robin Crossley, Isle of Wight County Press)
Right: Website announcement by Streatham Redhawks 2017

NIHL South - Division 1

Top Photo: South Division 1 champions Chelmsford Chieftains
Above left: Top points scorer Juraj Huska   Above right: Chieftains' netminders Sonny Phillips and Ben Clement
(All photos by Steve Sutherland www.icecoldphoto.co.uk)

NIHL South - Division 1

Final League Table – Division 1 South

Team	P	W	D	L	F	A	+/-	PIM	Pts
Chelmsford Chieftains	28	25	2	1	181	78	103	313	52
Invicta Dynamos	28	16	2	10	113	99	14	552	34
Streatham	28	15	2	11	94	86	8	579	32
Oxford City Stars	28	12	4	12	122	114	8	549	28
London Raiders S1	28	11	4	13	92	105	-13	566	26
Solent Devils	28	11	2	15	91	102	-11	347	24
Milton Keynes Thunder	28	9	2	17	91	125	-34	421	20
Bracknell Hornets	28	2	4	22	67	142	-75	466	8

Leading Points Scorers - 2016/17

Player	Team	GP	G	A	Pts	PIM
Juraj Huska	Chelmsford Chieftains	26	42	32	74	2
Adam ŘEhák	Invicta Dynamos	27	27	25	52	72
Daniel Hammond	Chelmsford Chieftains	27	28	23	51	18
Richard Facey	Solent Devils	28	21	27	48	48
Grant Bartlett	Chelmsford Chieftains	26	23	17	40	32
Cameron Bartlett	Chelmsford Chieftains	27	11	29	40	24
Aidan Doughty	Solent Devils	22	17	20	37	30
Callum Fowler	Invicta Dynamos	21	15	22	37	67
Alan Green	Oxford City Stars	28	18	19	37	83
Ashley Jackson	Invicta Dynamos	20	18	19	37	2

Leading Netminders 2016/17

Player	Team	GP	SA	GA	Sv%	SO
Damien King	Invicta Dynamos	10	330	23	93.03%	1
Sonny Phillips	Chelmsford Chieftains	23	357	26	92.72%	1
Ben Clements	Chelmsford Chieftains	27	620	51	91.77%	1
Christian Cole	Solent Devils	27	996	84	91.57%	0
Matthew Colclough	Streatham	23	694	65	90.63%	2
John Dibble	Invicta Dynamos	21	635	60	90.55%	1
Euan King	London Raiders	25	966	98	89.86%	2
Tom Annetts	Oxford City Stars	25	762	80	89.50%	2
Milan Ronai	Bracknell Hornets	12	123	13	89.43%	1
David Wride	Milton Keynes Thunder	28	1015	121	88.08%	0
Daniel Milton	Bracknell Hornets	28	844	101	88.03%	0
James Richardson	Invicta Dynamos	18	111	14	87.39%	2
Mark Duffy	Oxford City Stars	23	178	26	85.39%	1

Another year of hockey for the ever improving NIHL South Division 1 would see some familiar domination by one Essex-based team. However, that one team didn't have it all its own way as all the other 8 sides raised the bar and one of their rivals came good in the playoffs. Twinged with some sadness as one well known top 3 side was forced to fold early on, NIHL South 1 Editor Chris (Badger) Randall looks back on how all the sides season unfolded over the 2016/2017 campaign - and the sad demise of his hometown side early in the autumn.

NIHL South - Division 1

Bracknell Hornets - Regular Season

Player	GP	G	A	Pts	PIM
Ondrej Pekarik	7	11	15	26	32
Benjamin Ealey-Newman	26	14	8	22	82
Michal Oravec	13	11	11	22	18
Daniel Hughes	28	8	9	17	8
Conor Redmond	19	8	8	16	18
Brandon Miles	15	8	6	14	60
Joshua Thomas Martin	21	3	7	10	52
Jordan Lea Gregory	20	3	6	9	42
Kamil Kinkor	8	6	3	9	14
Stewart Tait	11	2	7	9	26
Tom Avery	18	1	6	7	6
Ryan Handisides	15	3	4	7	4
Joshua Ealey-Newman	26	2	3	5	6
Jaroslav Kucej	8	2	3	5	2
William Stead	28	2	3	5	12
Tom Fisher	28	1	3	4	24
Harvey Hind-Pitcher	26	0	4	4	24
Martyn Gray	28	0	3	3	22
Liam Underdown	22	0	3	3	43
Sam Cheema	11	1	1	2	29
Daniel Milton	28	0	2	2	0
Joshua Abbott	8	1	0	1	2
Christopher Leykam	9	0	1	1	2
Jack Baveystock	10	0	0	0	0
Daniel Fay	2	0	0	0	0
Nathan Lea Gregory	12	0	0	0	0
Harry Simon Harcup	7	0	0	0	0
Michael Krogh	7	0	0	0	4
Kevin Mcgurk	8	0	0	0	0
Luke Reynolds	1	0	0	0	31
Milan Ronai	12	0	0	0	2
Aleksei Sereda	3	0	0	0	0

Bracknell Hornets –
Notes by Chris Randall

Bracknell Hornets finished bottom of the league. Low budget and again playing in the shadow of higher League Bees the Hornets brought on the Junior players as much as they could.

Starting the year with Head Coach Gareth Cox, they ended the year as Player Danny Hughes took on the dual role midway point of the season.

Imports Michal Oravec and Kamil Kinkor joined despite both starting at Streatham. Kinkor ended the season hurt and hardly played.

Wightlink's demise brought in Nathan and Jordan Gregory and San Cheema to strengthen.

With Ben and Joshua Ealey-Newman and experienced defence man Stewart Tait all on board the club couldn't climb of the bottom and ended the season looking up at everyone else.

Dropping to NIHL 2 will be a good move for them this season going forward

Netminder Statistics – Regular Season

Netminder	GP	TOI	SA	GA	Sv%	SO
Milan Ronai	12	52	123	13	89.43%	1
Daniel Milton	28	41	844	101	88.03%	0
Nathan Lea Gregory	12	14	142	23	83.80%	0
Kevin Mcgurk	8	9	8	4	50.00%	0

Kevin Slyfield Photography

NIHL South - Division 1

Bracknell Hornets Team Photo by Kevin Slyfield Photography

Back Row (l to r); Harry Harcup, Will Stead, Conor Redmond, Michal Oravec, Josh E-Newman,Harvey Hind-Pitcher, Josh Martin, Chris Leykam, Tom Fisher, Middle Row: Danny Hughes, Jordan Gregory, Martyn Gray, Ben E-Newman, Milan Ronai,(nm) Front: Danny Milton (nm)

Kevin Slyfield Photography web page www.flick.com/photos/juniorbeesicehockey

Chelmsford Chieftains Team Photo by Steve Sutherland, Ice Cold Photography

Back Row (l to r): Cameron Bartlett, Grant Bartlett, Ross Brears, Daniel Hammond, Anthony Leone, Charlie Phillips, Olegs Lascenko, Juraj Huska. Front Row (l to r): Ben Clements, Sean Barry, Lukas Zatopek, Matt Turner, Euan King

www.icecoldphoto.co.uk
07910 692808
@icecoldphotos
www.facebook.com/icecoldphoto

NIHL South - Division 1

Chelmsford Chieftains - Regular Season

Player	GP	G	A	Pts	PIM
Juraj Huska	26	42	32	74	2
Daniel Hammond	27	28	23	51	18
Grant Bartlett	26	23	17	40	32
Cameron Bartlett	27	11	29	40	24
Jake Sylvester	28	19	16	35	2
Matthew Turner	28	11	24	35	14
Oliver Baldock	28	9	22	31	14
Liam Chong	24	9	18	27	4
Anthony Leone	28	7	12	19	14
Lukas Zatopek	26	5	14	19	36
Darren Brown	23	11	6	17	4
Brandon Ayliffe	27	2	9	11	16
Sean Barry	28	0	11	11	36
Alexander Staples	28	0	11	11	43
Callum Wells	23	2	4	6	14
Carl Graham	16	0	3	3	22
Sonny Phillips	23	0	3	3	4
Andrius Kaminskas	2	1	1	2	4
Ben Clements	27	0	1	1	2
Olegs Lascenko	3	1	0	1	4
Daniel Paul Wright	11	0	1	1	0
Billy Cyril Cook	1	0	0	0	0
Ryan Morgan	8	0	0	0	0
Charlie Phillips	1	0	0	0	0
Nathanael Williams	4	0	0	0	0

Chelmsford Chieftains Notes by Chris Randall

Essex powerhouse Chelmsford Chieftains finished the season dropping just 3 points in League play. 2 draws and a single loss over the 28 game season.

After playing for the Chieftains and also coaching the Junior sides he stepped up to become Head Coach back in 2015/2016. So if was a safe bet after the previous year's successes that Sean Easton would returned for his 2nd straight consecutive season at the helm.

Signing most of the previous year's team, a stingy net minding tandem of 30 year old Ben Clements and talented youngster Sonny Phillips (20) to go with a tight defence the goals against was again the lowest in the league .

Netminder Statistics – Regular Season

Netminder	GP	TOI	SA	GA	Sv%	SO
Sonny Phillips	23	59	357	26	92.72%	1
Ben Clements	27	59	620	51	91.77%	1

Cont'd…

When you have with the likes of veteran import Lukas Zatopek (39), steady blue liner Alex Staples (27), along with youngster Calum Wells (19), promoted from the Warriors, the back end was well stocked.

Sean Barry (23) returned with experienced Danny Wright covering any injuries . A familiar face in Lithuanian Andruis Kaminkas came in when Zatopek went down with injury .Carl Graham (33), and 25 year old utility player Liam Chong were added to replace the outgoing Phillips brothers Billy as Charlie before the midway point of the year.

Up front regulars, Captain Anthony Leone (34), led by example , defensive forwards Matt Turner and Gary Brown (27) stifled the opposition with their solid two way play. Brothers Cameron and Grant Bartlett scored plenty, dropped the gloves and general hacked the opposition off effectively. Silky skating forward Danny Hammond would play his final season in the Black and Gold.

Along with Warriors promotions for 19 year olds Brandon Ayliffe, Oliver Baldock, Olegs Lascenko and Jake Sylvester the speed and youth was a great help. Nathaniel Williams came out of a sabbatical too to add some muscle. They won the League at a canter as most would predict.

NIHL South - Division 1

Invicta Dynamos – Regular Season

Player	GP	G	A	Pts	PIM
Adam Rehák	27	27	25	52	72
Callum Fowler	21	15	22	37	67
Ashley Jackson	20	18	19	37	2
Arran Strawson	26	9	18	27	26
Steven Osman	22	8	12	20	4
Mason Jon Webster	24	6	12	18	109
Conor Redmond	4	8	8	16	18
Ondrej Zosiak	28	6	9	15	20
Bailey Wootton	26	8	6	14	40
Nicky Lewis	19	4	9	13	22
Elliott Dewey	26	1	9	10	28
Joshua Condren	22	2	7	9	16
Tom Ralph	26	2	7	9	47
Scott William Bailey	8	1	4	5	0
Adam Mcnicoll	15	1	1	2	6
Haydn Wootton	14	1	1	2	4
Bradley Gutridge	27	0	1	1	4
Harrison Lillis	22	0	1	1	65
Jarvis Mewett	27	1	0	1	4
Taylor Wootton	12	1	0	1	2
Anthony Baskerville	27	0	0	0	0
John Dibble	21	0	0	0	2
Damien King	10	0	0	0	0
James Richardson	18	0	0	0	0
Kieran Wyatt	1	0	0	0	0

Invicta Dynamos Notes by Chris Randall

Snapping at the heels and giving the Chieftains something to think about were Kent outfit Invicta Dynamos. Returning for his 12th consecutive season was Head non playing coach Kevin Parrish.

Damien King (26) was regarded as the starting netminder, the former Peterborough netminder proving a solid guy in the pipes at this level. James Richardson (24) added support.

Both missing time so the team added Bristol Pitbull John Dibble who came in and added some stellar play. Veteran Glen Rodbourne and teenager Kieran Wyatt dressed too.

In defence familiar faces Arran Strawson (30) returned for his 5th straight season. Former Basingstoke Bison Elliot Dewey (20) returned to Kent. As did Import Ondrej Zosiak (26) for a second season. Adam Mcnicoll (22) missed a chunk of time hurt. Harrison Lillis (23) thrived under increased ice time, occasionally dropping the gloves to add some fireworks.

Netminder Statistics – Regular Season

Netminder	GP	TOI	SA	GA	Sv%	SO
Damien King	10	29	330	23	93.03%	1
John Dibble	21	14	635	60	90.55%	1
James Richardson	18	13	111	14	87.39%	2

Cont'd...

Underrated but useful Jarvis Mewett (21) went about his role with minimal fuss. New comer Tommy Ralph (23) was a fan favourite coming in from Hull Pirates as a physical d-man

Up front the usual plethora of skilled forwards returned. Appointed Captain surprisingly to some, Callum Fowler (25) continued to rack up the goals. Hockey field star Ashley Jackson (29) was a revelation and added some scoring punch. Steve Osman (29) returned to finish the season as the Leagues highest point scorer after splitting the season with Oxford City Stars. Dependable Nicky Lewis (29) has made Kent his second home, and quietly went about his business. Toughness was brought in as former Haringey and Peterborough Phantom Mason Webster joined. Not one to shy away from the rough stuff.

Depth came as Anthony Baskerville (28) who has great speed, alongside regular Brad Guttridge (30), added respite to the top two lines. Joshua Condren (21), and Conor Redmond (22) added strength. Wootton brothers Hayden and Taylor (both 19), along with Bailey (20) all were full timers after coming through the Invicta Junior system.

New import Adam Rehak (24) didn't take long at all to acclimate himself to British hockey firing in goals left right and centre and even scrapping occasionally. So - good news that he's returning for the 2017/2018 Season!

Finally they added 20 year old Scott Bailey midway at the deadline to cover for injuries that hit the side.

Runners up with 2 draws and 10 losses from their 28 games saw them just snag 2nd place from Streatham by two points they couldn't quite get the upper hand on them pesky Chieftains. The going this time around of course will be a lot tougher this coming year.

NIHL South - Division 1

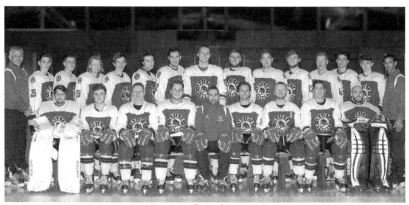

Invicta Dynamos Team Photo by David Trevallion

Back Row: (left to right): Asst Coach Kenny Redmond,Taylor Wootton, Jack Lee, Jacob Ranson, Connor Redmond, Joshua Condren, Steve Osman, Ondrej Zosiak, Jarvis Mewett, Damien Welch, Elliott Dewey, Brad Gutridge, Bailey Wootton, Hayden Wootton, Equipment Manager Martin Rider.
Front Row (left to right): Damien King, Andrew Henderson, Grant Baxter, Eriks Ozollapa, Head Coach Kevin Parrish, Nicky Lewis, Arran Strawson, Harrison Lillis, Steve Nightingale.

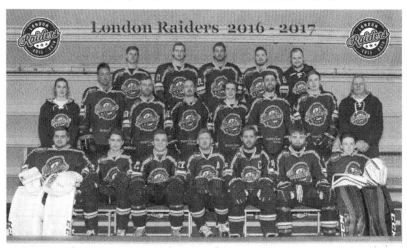

Andy Munroe · Slavomir Bada · Julian Smith · JJ Pitchley · Alan Blyth
Michelle Spight · Matt France (A) · Marek Nablik · Stewart Tait · Thomas Beesley · Sam Roberts · Jack Cooper · Kevin Davis
Euan King · Callum Burnett · Alan Lack · John Connolly (A) · Tom Davis (C) · Brandon Miles · Harry Buckingham

NIHL South - Division 1

London Raiders – Regular Season

Player	GP	G	A	Pts	PIM
Marek Nahlik	24	18	16	34	61
Jake J Pitchley	26	15	18	33	140
Slavomir Buda	26	14	12	26	12
Tom Davis	28	8	18	26	32
Thomas Beesley	27	7	11	18	12
Alan Lack	13	7	9	16	40
Brandon Miles	16	8	6	14	60
John Connolly	25	2	10	12	18
Jacob Ranson	14	3	8	11	24
Kamil Kinkor	2	6	3	9	14
Stewart Tait	20	2	7	9	26
James Pentecost	7	4	4	8	2
Sam Roberts	28	4	4	8	8
Ross Connolly	11	1	6	7	14
Matt France	23	0	6	6	33
Julian Smith	21	0	5	5	56
Jack Cooper	28	0	4	4	36
Andrew Munroe	11	0	3	3	10
Euan King	25	0	2	2	4
Callum Burnett	10	1	0	1	6
Bailey Chittock	9	1	0	1	6
Harry Buckingham	11	0	0	0	0
Michael Gray	9	0	0	0	10
Daniel y Lane	1	0	0	0	0
Jack Lee	2	0	0	0	2
Mark Robinson	5	0	0	0	0

London Raiders
Notes by Chris Randall

Raiders' 2016/2017 season was exactly a .500 record in points won and dropped. But, considering the bar has been raised in standards it could be viewed as a good season.

Returning Head Coach Alan Blyth had most of the roster return. Returnees included netminder Michael Gray, however he would leave mid-season and former Chelmsford Chieftain Euan King joined in his place to provide some solid goaltending.

They also had a netminder crisis, bringing in Ross Miller and Dan Lane from Bristol and Peterborough respectively when things went bad.

A strong defence with Julian Smith providing physical play and John Connolly, the latter missed a handful of games, the side noticed his absence but generally the back end was fairly solid.

Netminder Statistics – Regular Season

Netminder	GP	TOI	SA	GA	Sv%	SO
Michael Gray	9	0	132	8	93.94%	1
Euan King	25	24	966	98	89.86%	2
Daniel Ashley Lane	1	0	41	9	78.05%	0

Cont'd…

Up front, speedy Jacob Ranson created an effective forecheck. However several players either injured or leaving that was the story for the Gold and blue. Import Kamil Kinkor played just 2 games before heading to Bracknell then he suffered major injury. Slavomir Buda was his replacement with a point a game. But most felt he wasn't an upgrade on Kinkor. Marek Nahlik continued to give his all to the cause.

For the Brits, JJ Pitchley came up with points, big Brandon Miles - who joined from Bracknell - provided grit and would drop the gloves willingly and late additions veterans Stewart Tait and Andrew Munroe added experience at the deadline on the blue line.

All in all, the season can be viewed as a success, just not being able to consistently beat the top 4 was their downfall.

The 2017/2018 Season also suddenly got a lot harder with the collapse of the EPL. However, you can guarantee that whoever is wearing the Gold and Blue will give their all come September.

NIHL South - Division 1

Milton Keynes Thunder – Regular Season

Player	GP	G	A	Pts	PIM
Jakub Klima	27	19	16	35	12
Ross Bowers	21	13	16	29	38
Jamie Line	22	8	18	26	50
Ross Green	27	4	20	24	42
Harrison Goode	27	8	12	20	30
Tom Mboya	24	9	7	16	10
Cameron Wynn	15	4	11	15	2
Boris Ruzicka	23	7	5	12	34
Nick Chinn	12	1	10	11	18
Connor Goode	27	7	2	9	18
Hallden Barnes-Garner	9	5	1	6	4
Nidal Phillips	28	1	4	5	36
Alex Whyte	24	3	2	5	0
Adam Harris	19	1	2	3	0
James Clarke	20	1	1	2	4
Paul Gore	23	0	2	2	6
Simon Howard	8	1	0	1	12
Connor Hutchison	7	0	1	1	0
Greg Randall	14	0	1	1	2
Ryan Coffey	4	0	0	0	35
Christopher Jenkins	10	0	0	0	0
Nathan Long	1	0	0	0	0
Nicholas Poole	1	0	0	0	0
Jamie Randall	15	0	0	0	29
Luke Reynolds	9	0	0	0	31
Mark Woolf	10	0	0	0	0
David Wride	28	0	0	0	2

Milton Keynes Thunder Notes by Chris Randall

Always playing in the shadow of the EPL Lightning, Milton Keynes Thunder struggle to attract big crowds, which is a shame as they always play a high energy, heavy forechecking game and are always entertaining to watch.

Also they manage to attract some quality players, despite being one of the smallest budget teams in the League along with Solent and Bracknell.

Player Coach Paul Gore had returning veterans Simon Howard and Jamie Randall and Ross Bowers at his disposal.

Former long time Lightning Coach Nick Poole would play some games at the tail end of the season adding some leadership.

Netminder Statistics – Regular Season

Netminder	GP	TOI	SA	GA	Sv%	SO
David Wride	28	45	1015	121	88.08%	0
Mark Woolf	10	9	11	3	72.73%	0

Cont'd…

Regulars Nidal Phillips,Tom Mboya, Goode brothers Connor and Harrison gave the side some familiar faces. In net veteran Mark Woolf continued to give his all alongside David Wride

Defensively with Ross Green joining from the EPL as well as Cameron Wynn they had some good depth . Later in the season former Cardiff legend Nicky Chinn joined and took on the Player Coach role.

However the club couldn't climb any higher than 7th place in the standings. Even with a good import in Jakub Klima, and speedy centre Jamie Line, they found out how much the NIHL has improved as the season wore on.

No doubt they will find the going a lot tougher this season despite adding some significant players this off season

Milton Keynes Thunder Team Photo by Claire Stanton

Back Row (L to R): Adam Harris, Nick Poole, Alex Whyte, Cameron Wynn, James Clarke, Tom Mboya, Nidal Phillips, Ryan Coffey, Jakub Klima, Greg Randall, Jamie Randall
Front Row (L to R): David Wride (nm), Harrison Goode, Paul Gore, Ross Green (alternate captain), Jamie Line (captain), Ross Bowers (alternate captain), Connor Goode, Mark Woolf (nm)

Oxford City Stars Team Photo by Paul Foster

Back Row (l to r): Julie Anne Lacroix, Steven Caddick, Matt Jordan, Brendan Baird, Jaroslav Cesky, Mike Whillock, Josh Oliver, Ben Paynter, Jason Ikin, Ben Nethersell, Logan Prince, Josh Florey, Hallam Wilson, Phil Skaife, Simon Anderson. Front Row (l to r):Tom Annetts, Joe Oliver, Alan Green, Dominick Hopkins, Darren Elliott, Dax Hedges, Andrew Cox, Jake Florey, Joe Edwards and Mark Duffy.

NIHL South - Division 1

Player Statistics – Oxford City Stars – Regular Season

Player	GP	G	A	Pts	PIM	Oxford City Stars
Alan Green	28	18	19	37	83	**Notes by Chris Randall**
Jaroslav Cesky	21	10	21	31	62	
Dominic Hopkins	27	13	15	28	10	Headed up with keeping
Ondrej Pekarik	6	11	15	26	32	the Oxford City Stars in an
Joe Edwards	27	13	11	24	20	upward trajectory was
Benjamin Ealey-Newman	1	14	8	22	82	Head Coach Simon
Darren Elliott	15	5	15	20	27	Anderson. Coming in to
Joshua Oliver	26	8	10	18	12	take charge of his 5th
Brendan Baird	21	5	12	17	28	season (4th as Head
Ben Paynter	16	5	10	15	36	Coach) in between spells
Hallam Wilson	25	9	6	15	12	at other NIHL clubs in
Joshua Florey	26	6	8	14	34	recent years he's
Michael Whillock	24	5	9	14	56	improved teams wherever
Jesse River Lye	10	4	9	13	2	he's been.
Boris Ruzicka	2	7	5	12	34	Another season where he
Matt Jordan	26	2	7	9	6	took a team that most
Benjamin Nethersell	13	3	6	9	8	casual onlookers thought
Jake Florey	25	3	5	8	16	would be mid table, the
Dax Hedges	19	1	5	6	57	Oxford City Stars finished
Joshua Ealey-Newman	1	2	3	5	6	a credible 4th place finish
Joonas Liimatainen	13	3	1	4	2	just 4 points out of 3rd
Logan David Prince	14	0	3	3	0	place, and just 6 points
Joe Oliver	10	0	2	2	2	from runners up spot.
Tom Annetts	25	0	1	1	0	
Andrew Cox	13	1	0	1	10	Regulars such as Captain
Mark Duffy	23	0	1	1	2	Darren Elliot, Alan Green,
Jason William Ikin	24	1	0	1	30	Dax Hedges, Josh and
Aaron Burton	3	0	0	0	0	Joe Oliver saw some
Shannon Long	1	0	0	0	2	familiarity to the side.
Ryan Mcfarlane	2	0	0	0	0	
Grant Richardson	1	0	0	0	0	

Netminder Statistics – Regular Season

Netminder	GP	TOI	SA	GA	Sv%	SO
Tom Annetts	25	38	762	80	89.50%	2
Shannon Long	1	59	42	6	85.71%	0
Mark Duffy	23	18	178	26	85.39%	1

Cont'd…

The overseas contingent was a bit unsettled as first Slovak Boris Ruzicka only played 2 games before heading to Milton Keynes Thunder. Then Czech Ondrej Pekarik didn't last the year ending up at Bracknell Hornets. Tampere native from Finland Joonas Liimatainen ended the year as a key part of the puzzle.

After Wightlink's sad exit from the League, Stars picked up silky smooth skating Czech forward Jaroslav Cesky, gritty Ben Paynter and no nonsense defence man Brendan Baird to finish the season strongly down the stretch.

After deciding to drop to NIHL 2 for 2017/2018 Stars should be up there come September at the lower level, which seems a shame given their progression over the last couple of seasons.

NIHL South - Division 1

Player Statistics – Solent Devils – Regular Season

Player	GP	G	A	Pts	Pim
Richard Facey	28	21	27	48	48
Aidan Doughty	22	17	20	37	30
Alex Murray	28	9	25	34	26
Matthew Lawday	28	19	7	26	6
Mark Pitts	24	5	21	26	18
Andrew Campbell	13	6	6	12	2
Alexander Trendall	27	3	5	8	12
Mark Baroni	23	2	5	7	36
Mitchell Murray	6	2	4	6	33
Alexander Cole	25	0	5	5	24
Mason Wild	28	2	3	5	20
Sam Daniel Rudkin	26	2	2	4	6
Oliver Denis	21	0	3	3	12
Ben James Lock	18	1	2	3	20
Christian Cole	27	0	2	2	2
Montgomery Gailer	22	0	1	1	6
Kyle Goddard	5	1	0	1	2
Paul Petts	8	1	0	1	0
Hugo Tibbitts	13	0	1	1	4
Samuel Calder	19	0	0	0	0
Martin Clayton	5	0	0	0	0
Scott Greenfield	9	0	0	0	12
Christopher Hocquigny	2	0	0	0	0
Rhys Mc Cormick	5	0	0	0	0
Jacob Rondeau-Smith	16	0	0	0	0
Perry Stewart	18	0	0	0	2
Jacob Stoodley	7	0	0	0	0
Luke Richard Tull	24	0	0	0	14

Solent Devils
Notes by Chris Randall

A team that continues to make strides and did again in 2016/2017 was South coast outfit Solent Devils, coached by Player- Head Coach Alex Murray back for his 4th straight season.

The low budget side surprised many teams throughout the campaign, as teams quite often took them lightly and it backfired on them - just ask Invicta Dynamos!

Back in net was Christian (Chico) Cole, who once again performed miracles in net to keep the score line down.

Youngster Sam Calder didn't see a tonne of time in net as Cole iced in most of the games.

Netminder Statistics – Regular Season

Netminder	GP	TOI	SA	GA	Sv%	SO
Christian Cole	27	12	996	84	91.57%	0
Samuel James Calder	19	43	95	16	83.16%	0

.
Cont'd...

In defence, regulars Captain Alex Cole, and Ben Lock returned alongside former Oxford City Star Mason Wild. They also had American Import Mark Baroni hook up with the team who was solid defensively.

Up front, Coach Murray filled his lines as established Brit Richard Facey killed penalties and provided some offence. Coach Murray's younger brother Mitchell was also a threat however some unsavoury moments where controversial actions from a home game saw his season end abruptly .

Mark Pitts joined from NIHL 2 side Basingstoke Buffalo and was a good addition up front. Speed came from former Wightlink youngster Alex Trendall who returned for a 2nd season and improved over the year.

Another that improved the team's fortunes was top Brit Aiden Doughty. The former Wightlink hotshot was a menace for opposition defences as his skill and physical play was a very welcome boost when he joined after Raiders demise.

All in all, some great home results including a walloping against Invicta Dynamos and a huge 4 point haul that weekend showed what the Devils were capable of.

The team made the decision to drop to NIHL 2 for the 2017/2018 season. Given the vast improvement that NIHL 1 will see, the lower level is the best move financially and competitively for the long-term future of the South Coast side.

NIHL South - Division 1

Solent Devils Team Photo by Dave Chapman

Standing (left to right): Martin Clayton, Graham Cole, Jacob Rondeau-Smith, Alex Trendall, Perry Stewart, Hugo Tibbitts, Ben Lock, Mitchell Murray, Monty Gailer, Mark Baroni Aidan Doughty, Paul Petts, Mark Pitts, Sam Rudkin, Kyle Goddard, Luke Tull, Rhys McCormick, Paul Fitzpatrick, James Morgan, Denise Ferguson

Sitting (left to right): Jake Stoodley, Matt Lawday, Richard Facey, Alex Murray, Christian Cole, Alex Cole, Mason Wild, Oliver Dennis, Sam Calder

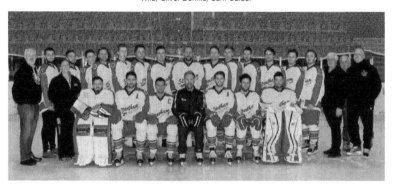

Streatham Redhawks Team Photo by Rick Webb

Back Row (l to r): Bill Webb (asst coach), Daniel Clayton, Joe Allen, Ryan Webb, Vaclav Drabek, George Norcliffe, Chris Cooke, Ryan Giles, Jack Tarzyckie , Steve Fisher, Alex Sampford, Sean Scarbrough, Danny Rose, James Warman, Callum Best, Manager Graham D`Anger. Kit Manager Don Young, Asst Coach Terry England.

Front Row (l to r) : Physio Tanya Romans. Netminder Will Sanderson. Caz Britton, Joe Johnston, Coach Jeremy Cornish, Adam Wood, Liam Rasmussen, Netminder Matt Colclough

NIHL South - Division 1

Player Statistics – Streatham Redhawks – Regular Season

Player	GP	G	A	Pts	PIM
Callum Best	26	13	22	35	34
Sean Scarbrough	28	16	13	29	4
George Norcliffe	23	15	7	22	10
Michal Oravec	6	11	11	22	18
Steven Fisher	27	6	11	17	71
Alexander Sampford	17	8	9	17	2
Conor Redmond	2	8	8	16	18
Ryan Webb	23	6	9	15	0
Adam Wood	26	6	8	14	125
Nick Chinn	4	1	10	11	18
Jacob Ranson	10	3	8	11	24
Joseph Johnston	26	2	8	10	28
Daniel Rose	20	3	6	9	4
Casimir Madren-Britton	26	0	8	8	20
Joe Allen	25	3	4	7	8
Vaclav Drabek	7	1	6	7	18
James Warman	28	2	4	6	16
Christopher Cooke	20	2	3	5	8
Ryan Giles	22	1	4	5	44
Jack Tarczycki	23	1	3	4	24
Liam Rasmussen	27	2	1	3	39
Euan King	5	0	2	2	4
David Savage	3	1	1	2	32
Christopher Wiggins	4	1	1	2	34
Daniel Clayton	10	0	0	0	0
Matthew Colclough	23	0	0	0	4
Nick Compton	2	0	0	0	2
Jack Lee	2	0	0	0	2
Adam Mahoney	1	0	0	0	0
Stefan Nubert	4	0	0	0	0
William Sanderson	13	0	0	0	0
Conor Sheehan	3	0	0	0	0
Brett Shepherd	8	0	0	0	0

Streatham Red Hawks notes by Chris Randall

SW16 was a happier place come April as a team that has always caused shock results has never really challenged for the League title, the start of the season looked no different . Mid table looked to be best they would offer.

However, with the sad demise of Wightlink Raiders after losing their rink, Streatham underwent two major changes.

The first was the dropping of the Redskins tag that has been synonymous with the South London side for some 40 years and a fans poll decided on the RedHawks moniker instead .

The icing on the cake came in the form of Wightlink's Head Coach Jeremy Cornish -the Lucan, Ontario, native widely regarded as one of the best coaches in the League.

He added some 7/8 of his Wightlink team and changed the dynamic of the side in the months ahead.

Regulars such as Casmir Madren-Britton and team Captain Joe Johnston were regarded as the heartbeat of the team and they suddenly became a top 3 side

Netminder Statistics – Regular Season

Netminder	GP	TOI	SA	GA	Sv%	SO
Christopher D.C. Cooke	20	0	31	0	100.00%	1
Matthew Colclough	23	30	694	65	90.63%	2
Euan King	5	24	966	98	89.86%	2
William Sanderson	13	58	29	6	79.31%	0

American Import Sean Scarborough and top Brit Callum Best was a deadly combo up front . Mixed in with top netminder Matty Colclough and a strengthened D core with the likes of Nick Compton and the speedy checking of Joe Allen the RedHawks nearly snatched a runners up place. This of course all too familiar with Coach Cornish - always looking up at the Essex rivals the Chieftains.

Heading into next season one would think with Chelmsford playing in NIHL 2, things might come good, but with the demise of the EPL Streatham will still have their work cut out at the top.

NIHL South - Division 1

Player Statistics – Wightlink Raiders
Up To 24th October 2017 only

Player	League					South 1 Cup				
	GP	G	A	Pts	PIM	GP	G	A	Pts	PIM
Aidan Doughty	4	1	3	4	4	4	1	3	4	6
Alexander Sampford	4	1	1	2	0	4	3	4	7	0
Ben Paynter	1	0	2	2	2	3	0	1	1	54
Brendan Baird	4	2	1	3	4	4	0	3	3	16
Christopher D.C. Cooke	4	0	1	1	2	4	1	1	2	6
Corey Watkins	1	0	0	0	6	3	1	2	3	51
Daniel Rose	4	0	3	3	4	4	3	2	5	4
Daniel William Shier	1	0	0	0	0	1	0	0	0	4
Danny Oliver Ingoldsby	2	2	0	2	0	3	0	2	2	4
George Brian Norcliffe	4	1	2	3	0	4	1	5	6	2
Jaroslav Cesky	4	0	5	5	2	4	4	2	6	4
Jeremy Cornish	0	0	0	0	0	1	0	0	0	0
Jordan Lea Gregory	4	1	1	2	4	4	1	1	2	4
Matthew Colclough	4	0	0	0	0	4	0	0	0	0
Nathan Lea Gregory	4	0	0	0	0	4	0	0	0	0
Nick Compton	4	0	0	0	0	4	0	1	1	4
Richard Nembhard	2	1	0	1	0	2	0	0	0	0
Ryan Webb	4	4	0	4	0	4	5	1	6	4
Sam Cheema	4	0	0	0	6	4	0	1	1	0
Vaclav Drabek	4	0	0	0	6	3	4	0	4	0

Netminder Statistics – Wightlink Raiders
Up To 24th October 2017 only

	League					South 1 Cup				
	GP	SA	GA	SA%	SO	GP	SA	GA	SA%	SO
Matthew Colclough	4	148	17	88.51%	0	4	104	9	91.35%	0
Nathan Lea Gregory						4	40	5	87.50%	1

Raiders Report by Chris Randall

Head Coach Jeremy Cornish looked to have signed a strong side with some key additions and pivotal returnees. However the script went disastrously wrong through no fault of their own.

The trust that ran the rink was effectively frozen out of the building just a short time into the season, over problems with rent, and building work not being completed at all, after an alleged insurance payout to have the work done. So bit by bit the dynasty and winning mentality that Jeremy Cornish had instilled on the island - not to mention a League and Playoff Championship his time there was all undone overnight.

A credit to Cornish and the players and opposition clubs that every single one of the Wightlink side was picked up by other clubs - mainly Bracknell, Oxford and in particular Streatham gaining the most with some 7/8 players and Cornish himself headed to SW16 to take up the Head Coach role in the Capital, they all managed to save their seasons.

NIHL South - Division 1

Interior view of the Isle of Wight Arena in happier times

Wightlink Raiders Team – last game at Invicta (Photo by David Trevallion)
Back Row (L to R): Aiden Doughty, Brendan Baird, Dan Rose, Mathew Colclough, Corey Watkins, Richard Nembhard, Alex Sampford, Christopher Cooke, (Head Coach) Jeremy Cornish, Team Director Steve Price, Ryan Webb, George Norcliffe. Front Row (L to R): Sam Cheema, Nathan Gregory, Benjamin Paynter, Jordan Gregory, Danny Ingoldsby, Nick Compton, Jaroslav Cesky.

(Cont'd...)

However, the losers in all this were the Isle of Wight faithful who have grown to love their side since they were originally set up back in 1991 as Solent Vikings.

A crying shame that, despite the building still standing over a year on, and empty with no new tenants it's a sad state of affairs for the hockey community and the Islands loyal fan base. No one knows if there is a future for the game on the island, given their big crowds it is a travesty for them.

NIHL South - Division 1

Invicta Dynamos celebrate winning the South 1 Play Off Final with a 10-7 aggregate win over Chelmsford
(Photo by David Trevallion)

Chelmsford Chieftains with the South 1 Cup that they won after a two legged final win against Invicta Dynamos.
(Photo by Steve Sutherland - www.icecoldphoto.co.uk).

NIHL South Division 1 Play Offs

NIHL South Division 1 Play Offs – Final

1st Leg – 8th April 2017	2nd Leg – 9th April 2017	Aggregate Score
Dynamos 8 – Chieftains 3	Chieftains 4 – Dynamos 2	Dynamos win 10-7

NIHL South Division 1 Play Offs – Semi Finals

1st Leg – 1st April 2017	2nd Leg – 2nd April 2017	Aggregate Score
(Lon) Raiders 1 – Chieftains 5	Chieftains 11 – Raiders 3	Chieftains win 16-4
Streatham 3 - Dynamos 3	Dynamos 10 - Streatham 1	Dynamos win 13-4

NIHL South Division 1 Play Offs – Quarter Finals

1st Leg 25th March 2017	2nd Leg 26th March 2017	Aggregate Score
Dynamos 3 - MK Thunder 1	MK Thunder 5 – Dynamos 6	Dynamos win 9-6
Hornets 2 - Chieftains 4	Chieftains 6 – Hornets 2	Chieftains win 10-4
(Lon) Raiders 4 – Stars 2	Stars 1 – Raiders 7	Raiders win 11-3
Devils 2 - Streatham 2	Streatham 3 – Devils 2	Streatham win 5-4

NIHL South Division 1 Cup

NIHL South Division 1 Cup – Final

1st Leg – 18th March 2017	2nd Leg – 19th March 2017	Aggregate Score
Chieftains 4 – Dynamos 3	Dynamos 2 – Chieftains 4	Chieftains win 8-5

NIHL South Division 1 Cup – Semi Finals

1st Leg – 25th February 2017	2nd Leg – 26th February 2017	Aggregate Score
(Lon) Raiders 2 – Chieftains 3	Chieftains 5 – Raiders 0	Chieftains win 8-2
Streatham 2 - Dynamos 7	Dynamos 5 - Streatham 2	Dynamos win 13-4

South 1 Cup – Group Table							
Team	P	W	D	L	GF	GA	Pts
Invicta Dynamos	6	5	0	1	27	19	10
London Raiders	6	3	1	2	26	22	7
Chelmsford Chieftains	6	2	0	4	16	20	4
Streatham Redhawks	6	1	1	4	15	23	3

South 1 BBO Cup – Group Table							
Team	P	W	D	L	GF	GA	Pts
Milton Keynes Thunder	4	3	1	0	18	8	7
Oxford City Stars	4	1	1	2	14	20	3
Bracknell Hornets	4	0	2	2	9	13	2

The South 1 Cup continued as a 4-team group after Wightlink Raiders were forced to drop out. All 4 teams consequently qualified for the semi- finals.

The BBO Cup was organised between Bracknell, Oxford and Milton Keynes to provide extra games for those teams after Cardiff Devils dropped out of South 1. It was played on a group basis only and Thunder's top place finish brought them their first trophy for 15 years. .

NIHL South

Above: Cesky as a Peterborough Phantom in the EPL (Photo by Tom Scott - AMO Images)
Below: Last season with Oxford City Stars (Photo by Paul Foster) & On the Isle of Wight with Raiders' coach Jeremy Cornish reading Ice Hockey Review (Photo by Chris Randall)

JAROSLAV CESKY - Interview by Chris Randall

The name Jaroslav Cesky is a well known name in British hockey circles having first came to the Uk for the Bracknell Bees in 2009 , with spells at Swindon Wildcats, Telford Tigers, Basingstoke Bison, Peterborough Phantoms as well as time in the Elite League with Cardiff Devils, Edinburgh Capitals he's been a favourite wherever he has iced over his time in the UK. I put him under the spotlight ... And here's what he had to say ....

At what age did you learn to skate ?, and who was responsible for getting you to take the game up ?.
I started playing hockey when I was 6 years old. My brother is year older then me and he got invited to play ice hockey and I came along, we played together until about 12. My parents always supported me in hockey and the brought me to every practice and games. I am very thankful for it.

Did you go the usual junior route, and where and when did you make your senior debut ? .
I played in Czech all the way to junior, my two final years of junior hockey I had the opportunity to go to USA, and play there, my last year junior I played USHL, in Dubuque fighting saints, and got recruited to NCAA college, I end up getting scholarship to Augsburg college and end up getting my BA in international business.

After college I end up played my in the UHL my first professional season for Adirondacks ice hawks, next 3 seasons I played in the Chl, last year I played in the IHL, flint generals.

Playing in your homeland, did you have a favourite player growing up that you looked up to and idolised ?.
Growing up I always liked obvious famous Czech hockey star Jaromir JAGR. He's was always the guy I supported and enjoyed watching.

Who was it and how did you come to play in the Uk back in 2009/2010 season ?
After my USA career I wanted to play little closer to home so I end up playing next between season in France, league Magnus for team Chamonix great experience and great place to play. Season after that I contacted a few agents they found me Bracknell bees.

You had a prolific partnership with Michal Pinc. What was it like playing alongside him and no doubt it was a fun experience ? .Do you still keep in touch with him ? .
Claude Dumas was the coach and he ask if I knew any players and I recommended Michal Pinc. We played together for a month or so in France and I really enjoyed playing with him, and we end up playing together for 3 year in the uk.

I introduced him to his wife and they now have beautiful girl together. We're still friends, and try to see each other as much as we can. Michal no longer played ice hockey, he works on the boats and travels Europe as a sailor.

You dropped down into the NIHL a few years ago, how do find the League and the improvement it's seems to be showing year on year ? .
NIHL is definitely getting better each year, now with the NIHL combining with EPL it will be interesting how the hockey will shape up.

No announcement in you playing this coming season, what does the future hold for you and will you get into coaching when you do hang them up ? .
I will be playing again somewhere next year, just wait and see where I end ip .As far as me playing, I go by year by year, every season and game I treat as it could be my last one I ever play on competitive level so, I train, play as hard as I can. That is also how I live my life.

I have a son now called Jaroslav Český. Exactly same as me!!! One day you will see him skate around on the ice. I will be the first coach that he will ever have that's for sure.:-)

NIHL South

MEET THE REF:
Rene Ross

By
NIHL South Editor
Chris Randall

< *Referee Rene Ross in action*
Photo by Flyfifer Photography
(www.flyfifer.co.uk)

When did you first learn to skate, and did you get into playing the game?

I first put skates on in the old Southampton rink when I was 12 but I can't say I really started skating properly till I was 16, me and friends would jump on a train and go down to Southampton on a regular basis for session skates.

I also remember myself and a couple of friends (the only ones in Basingstoke to have skates) skating on a frozen boating lake one year for a couple of months , I did not get to play hockey until the Basingstoke rink opened but by then I was already 21 so a career as a player was out, so it was just rec hockey.

When and where did you first become involved into team stripes ?

I first got involved in hockey when I worked at Basingstoke rink when it first opened, Basingstoke only had a junior and senior team there in the first year but they still needed refs and Don Yewchin coaxed me into going over to Bracknell to a referee seminar and, 29 years later, I am still here.

Of all the officials do you have a favourite you like working with ?

That's a tough one as I have worked with so many over the years. Generally speaking, it's the guys I came up through the ranks with as linesmen but as you change to referees, you simply don't work together anymore. I enjoy working everyone and get a real kick from working with younger officials that are prepared listen and learn - Tom Pering being one of them. Tom worked as a linesman for me for many years and always asked about his performance on the car journeys home from games and how he could improve.

What the highest level you have officiated in your career ?

I guess the answer is the top level as I refereed in the Heineken League years - which I think many people see as the best time of British hockey as it was not split into separate competitions. I do miss the Wembley finals weekend with fans from every club in the country in attendance - it was a true family atmosphere.

NIHL South

Several years ago, we lost a great ambassador for the sport in Dave Tottman. Did that hit the refs and linos hard when that tragedy occurred ?

During my career we have had two massive referee family losses. The first was Mickey Curry and the second being Dave. Both losses hit the referees badly as it did many players whose lives these guys had touched, Dave's passing re-enforced my beliefs that hockey is a family, the out-pouring of emotion from not only team stripes but from the hockey community at large was heartfelt (still miss him now).

His daughter Joy is a well-respected official and has achieved so much. Does that make the officiating crew for Ice Hockey give you a sense of admiration for her?

Joy has always been an great person to work with and I know many referees were very proud of how far she has gone (you can't really get much higher than doing an Olympic Final), But things have changed now and she has hung up her skates and she will drive to improve referee standards in the UK with her leadership - I simply call her "boss".

You have recently been abroad... have you officiated overseas much in your career ?

I have been away with the IHUK In-line hockey team at the IIHF world championships as the team manager, I fell into the management role after refereeing for 5 years at world championship level, the standard of play is unbelievable with many teams having ex and current NHL players in their squads basically playing ice hockey on wheels for fun.

Do you think Dave Cloutman is the model of professionalism with his longevity in the game and is he a guy some younger newer officials look to for advice, along with yourself ?

As myself and Dave have been around for a long time (me 29 years and Dave 33 years) we like to think we show some degree of professionalism in how we do things and we do both enjoy encouraging newer younger officials, I know that was true for me when I was developing as an official and many new officials could learn a lot from just simply asking questions, I have a golden rule: " there are no stupid questions just stupid answers".

What's been the highlight in your career to date ?

I think there is not one highlight but 29 years of great moments, refereeing the Junior final at Wembley, skating out in front of 10,000 in Sheffield in the first season when the next largest gate during that era was 3,500, doing a game that was broadcast on the BBC Grandstand on Saturday afternoon, and a great highlight has been to be on the ice with so many great players watching them do their thing from the best vantage point in the rink.

Do you have other roles within ice hockey?

I have been a trustee for the Ice Hockey Players Benevolent Fund since its inception back in 1996, our role is to financially support any player coach or referee who is in need, whether it be from an illness or injury.

How do you feel about the recent the changes to the UK senior leagues and the direction the UK is headed?

Well, I like to think this a dawn of a new era, and with strong leadership from IHUK it will happen. We can stamp out the boom and bust attitudes from clubs and owners which will make UK hockey a great place to play in. It will produce a great game to watch and bring stability to clubs, limiting imports can only help with stability and also help the national team as it will give British players the opportunity to play more.

As for referees, we have already started on our path to improving standards, progression and learning by putting together a new way of working, and that is the reason why I have skated my last game as my mission now will be to help out our pool of referees.

NIHL South Division 2

Bristol Pitbulls v Peterborough Islanders in the South 2 Cup group stage. For the Cup competition, the Pitbulls wore a nostalgic green kit in recognition of the famous Avon Arrows team who played at Bristol from 1974 to 1982. (Photo by Flyfifer Photography – www.flyfifer.co.uk)

NIHL South Division 2 Review
by NIHL South Editor Chris Randall

The lowest tier of League hockey, the NIHL 2 continued with its East/West Conference format. The East with 6 teams playing 20 games. The West with 5 teams playing 16 games.

It was the story of Peterborough Islanders storming the East Conference without losing a game and only dropping 1 point to become Conference winners.

Last year's Champions Chelmsford Warriors losing several players to NIHL 1 side Chieftains would mean they weren't as dominant this time around with 2 draws and 6 losses.

There were improved seasons from Invicta Mustangs and Lee Valley Lions, with Haringey Racers and Slough Jets fortunes dipping somewhat. The League continued to provide a platform to blood youngsters which had been the Chelmsford Warriors catalyst for success.

Into the West, and Cardiff Fire picked up from the year before - steam rolling their way to the West Conference title without losing all season. 14 and 0, they had a strong side. Richie Hargreaves' Bristol Pitbulls managed 7 wins, the nearest challengers, with Wightlink Buccaneers bravely continuing despite the loss of their rink.

Basingstoke Buffalo and Swindon NIHL Wildcats battled bravely but only managed just 3 wins each - it was a lot tougher at the bottom.

Cardiff Fire have now been promoted to South Division 1 which will be a tougher test with the changes there, and they have also set up a new South 2 as well.

Peterborough Islanders - now directly affiliated with the Phantoms – shows a natural pathway in the Fens and should see interesting seasons ahead for both of the South 2 top 2 from last season.

NIHL SOUTH DIVISION 2 West – FINAL LEAGUE TABLE 2016/17

NIHL S2 West	P	W	D	L	F	A	+/-	PIM	Pts
Cardiff Fire South	14	14	0	0	91	24	67	344	32*
Bristol Pitbulls	15	7	3	5	72	55	17	374	19*
Wightlink Buccaneers	10	3	1	6	29	54	-25	146	11*
Basingstoke Buffalo	14	3	2	9	44	77	-33	150	10*
Swindon Wildcats	15	3	2	10	61	87	-26	246	8

Note: Wightlink Buccaneers played games away for double points after their home rink closed in September 2016.

Top Points Scorers – 2016/17

Player	Team	GP	G	A	Pts	PIM
Robert Sedlak	Cardiff Fire	14	13	11	24	22
Tamas Elias	Cardiff Fire	14	14	9	23	4
Jordan Powell	Cardiff Fire	12	9	14	23	38
Loris Taylor	Swindon Wildcats	13	12	11	23	10
Olly Shone	Bristol Pitbulls	13	11	9	20	22
Adam Coakley	Swindon Wildcats	15	10	9	19	28
Blair Dubyk	Wightlink Buccaneers	9	8	10	18	22
Paul Petts	Basingstoke Buffalo	13	6	12	18	16
Giacomo Raffaelli	Bristol Pitbulls	12	9	9	18	44
Samual Bryant	Cardiff Fire South	14	5	12	17	44
Jordan Peter Smith	Swindon Wildcats	15	9	8	17	12
Adrian Smith	Bristol Pitbulls	14	9	8	17	10
Michael Joseph Power	Swindon Wildcats	6	9	7	16	4

Top Netminders – 2016/17

Player	Team	GP	TOI	SA	GA	Sv%	SO
Luke Takel	Cardiff Fire	12	0	234	13	94.44%	1
Joseph Myers	Cardiff Fire	12	59	192	11	94.27%	0
John Dibble	Bristol Pitbulls	4	40	120	11	90.83%	0
Aaron Craft	Wightlink Buccaneers	10	59	557	54	90.31%	0
Aaron Burton	Bristol Pitbulls	3	21	10	1	90.00%	0
Andrew Leckie	Bristol Pitbulls	11	59	81	9	88.89%	1
Liam Mcguire	Swindon Wildcats	14	20	344	39	88.66%	0
Ross Miller	Bristol Pitbulls	10	52	283	34	87.99%	0
Samuel Calder	Basingstoke Buffalo	13	57	439	59	86.56%	0
Graeme Bird	Swindon Wildcats	14	38	343	48	86.01%	0
Kevin Mcgurk	Basingstoke Buffalo	10	0	93	16	82.80%	0

NIHL South Division 2 – Western Conference

Above: Cardiff Fire celebrate receiving the South 2 West League Trophy
(Photo by Nathan Munkley Photography)

Top Scorer: Cardiff Fire's Robert Sedlak.   *Cardiff Fire's Luke Takel was top netminder*

(Both Photos by Nathan Munkley Photography)

NIHL South Division 2 – Western Conference

Basingstoke Buffalo - Player Statistics – Regular Seaso

Player	GP	G	A	Pts	PIM
Paul Petts	13	6	12	18	16
Warren Jones	13	6	7	13	18
Gregory Martyn	13	5	7	12	0
Mark Austen	13	3	7	10	14
Joseph Denness	12	5	5	10	16
Kyle David Goddard	11	1	5	6	16
Connor Hutchison	13	4	2	6	14
Cameron Edward Buckle	12	2	3	5	4
Michael Gorman	13	4	1	5	6
Andrew Pickles	4	2	3	5	6
Samuel Jordan Brooks	10	3	1	4	2
Sam Dollin	11	0	4	4	6
Josh Lewis Edwin Richards	10	1	1	2	4
David Collins	2	1	0	1	0
Samuel Compton	10	0	1	1	4
Neil Leary	8	0	1	1	12
Liam Poulson	13	0	1	1	0
Jack George Standing	11	1	0	1	2
Samuel James Calder	13	0	0	0	2
Matthew Friend	2	0	0	0	0
Matthew James Levy	1	0	0	0	4
Rhys James Mc Cormick	6	0	0	0	0
Kevin Mcgurk	10	0	0	0	0
Jake Anthony Wadge	5	0	0	0	0

Basingstoke Buffalo – Netminder Statistics

Player	GP	TOI	SA	GA	Sv%	SO
Samuel James Calder	13	57	439	59	86.56%	0
Kevin Mcgurk	10	0	93	16	82.80%	0

NIHL South Division 2 – Western Conference

Bristol Pitbulls - Player Statistics – Regular Season

Player	P	G	A	Pts	PIMs
Olly Shone	13	11	9	20	22
Giacomo Raffaelli	12	9	9	18	44
Adrian Smith	14	9	8	17	10
Jamie Newton	11	4	11	15	0
Joshua Dolphin	13	7	5	12	8
Logan David Prince	14	5	7	12	4
Grant Richardson	12	5	7	12	16
Ryan Mcfarlane	12	1	7	8	40
Giovanni Raffaelli	9	4	4	8	12
Thomas Asprey	13	2	4	6	6
Michael Hargreaves	11	2	4	6	30
Richard Hargreaves	11	3	3	6	69
Joshua Jack Galea	14	2	3	5	8
Christopher Moore	14	2	3	5	8
Zachary Dolphin	12	1	3	4	2
Sam Shone	12	2	2	4	42
Janne Virtanen	13	1	3	4	4
Jordan Jefferies	13	1	2	3	10
Daniel John Murrells	13	0	2	2	2
Tom Egerton	3	1	0	1	0
Aaron Burton	3	0	0	0	0
Macaulay Coppock	2	0	0	0	0
John Dibble	4	0	0	0	0
Andrew Leckie	11	0	0	0	4
Ross Miller	10	0	0	0	0
Matthew Thornhill	9	0	0	0	31

Bristol Pitbulls Netminder Statistics

Player	GP	TOI	SA	GA	Sv%	SO
John Dibble	4	40	120	11	90.83%	0
Aaron Burton	3	21	10	1	90.00%	0
Andrew Leckie	11	59	81	9	88.89%	1
Ross Miller	10	52	283	34	87.99%	0

NIHL South Division 2 – Western Conference

Bristol Pitbulls Team Photo by Flyfifer Photography (www.flyfifer.co.uk)
Back Row (l to r): Janne Virtanen, Josh Galea, Jordan Smith, Sam Shone, Olly Smith, Adrian Smith, Mac Coppock, Zach Dolphin, Logan Prince, Matt Thornhill
Front row (l to r): Steve Couzens (ass coach), Andy Leckie, Chris Moore, Yousif Abu Saada, Dan Pettitt (A), Tom Asprey (C), Grant Richardson (A), Richie Hargreaves (player/coach), Josh Dolphin, John Dibble

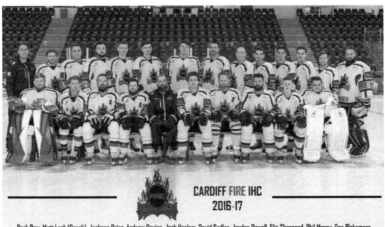

CARDIFF FIRE IHC
2016-17

Back Row: Matt Lock (Coach), Jackson Price, Andrew Davies, Josh Haslam, David Sadler, Jordan Powell, Elis Sheppard, Phil Manny, Dan Blakemore, Chris Hart,Tomas Elias, Niall Shanahan, Dan Self, Joe Myers

Front Row: Luke Takel, David Christian, Robert Sedlak (A), Ricky Deacon (A), Mark Cuddihy (Coach), Tim Burrows (C), Ross Wilkinson (A), Alan Armour, Sam Bryant, James Whiting

NIHL South Division 2 – Western Conference

Cardiff Fire – Player Statistics – Regular Season

Player	P	G	A	Pts	PIMs
Robert Sedlak	14	13	11	24	22
Tamas Elias	14	14	9	23	4
Jordan Powell	12	9	14	23	38
Samual Bryant	14	5	12	17	44
Jackson Lewis Price	14	7	7	14	30
Sam Smith	9	8	6	14	4
Ross Wilkinson	13	3	11	14	24
David Sadler	13	2	11	13	37
Alan Armour	14	4	7	11	8
Tim Burrows	6	4	4	8	27
David Christian	14	6	2	8	10
Andrew Davies	14	0	7	7	8
Stephen Deacon	10	6	1	7	12
Josh Elwyn Haslam	12	5	2	7	4
Philip Manny	14	0	7	7	22
Christopher Hart	11	0	6	6	8
Daniel Blakemore	4	1	3	4	0
Elis John Sheppard	14	2	1	3	12
Jordan Baber	11	0	2	2	4
Jonathan Nash	2	1	1	2	2
Daniel Self	13	0	2	2	0
Niall Shanahan	10	1	1	2	0
Kieran Latchford	4	0	1	1	0
Joe Morris	6	0	1	1	4
Joseph Myers	12	0	1	1	16
Steve Newton	1	0	0	0	0
Luke Takel	12	0	0	0	0
James Michael Whiting	7	0	0	0	2

Cardiff Fire – Netminder Statistics

Player	GP	TOI	SA	GA	Sv%	SO
Luke Takel	12	0	234	13	94.44%	1
Joseph Myers	12	59	192	11	94.27%	0

Nathan Munkley
—*Photography*—
nmunkleyphotography.com
 nmunkleyphotography

NIHL South Division 2 – Western Conference

Swindon NIHL Wildcats Player Statistics – Regular Season

Player	P	G	A	Pts	PIMS
Loris Taylor	13	12	11	23	10
Adam Coakley	15	10	9	19	28
Jordan Peter Smith	15	9	8	17	12
Michael Joseph Power	6	9	7	16	4
Nathan John Chilcott	15	5	6	11	8
Daniel Sullivan	13	2	5	7	4
Deakan Luke Fielder	6	3	3	6	6
Lee Michael Beardsmore	14	4	0	4	0
William James Harding	13	1	3	4	10
Ilija Kolosnicins	6	1	3	4	8
Kaine Collins	13	0	3	3	6
Adam Matthew Finlinson	1	0	3	3	0
Daniel Pettitt	11	1	2	3	26
Stuart Widdows	11	0	3	3	48
Yousif Abu Saada	5	1	1	2	14
Ryan Aldridge	2	0	2	2	2
Jordan Paul Kelsall	2	1	1	2	2
Graeme Bird	14	0	1	1	10
Jaeden Boland-Pedley	12	0	1	1	4
Jack Clark	7	0	1	1	0
Joshua Francis Kelly	6	1	0	1	0
Haydn Nathan Lee	13	0	1	1	6
Luke Merrick	13	0	1	1	18
Harvey Robson	5	0	1	1	6
Daniel Williams	2	1	0	1	0
Andrew Coakley	13	0	0	0	6
Liam Mcguire	14	0	0	0	2

Swindon NIHL Wildcats Netminder Statistics – Regular Season

Netminder	GP	TOI	SA	GA	Sv%	SO
Liam Mcguire	14	20	344	39	88.66%	0
Graeme Bird	14	38	343	48	86.01%	0

NIHL South Division 2 – Western Conference

Wightlink Buccaneers 2016/17

In photo: Aaron Craft, Andrew Robinson, Andy Shier, Blair Dubyck, Corey Watkins, Dan Shier, Drew McCluskey, Harry Brown, Joe Osborne, Justin Attrill, Kieran Annis, Kurt Tyrell, Marcus Russell, Mike Palin, Mitchell Brown, Nathan Webb, Ricky Attrill, Sean Richardson, Shaun Harris.

 graham@flyfifer.co.uk   flyfifer.photography   @flyfiferphoto

NIHL South Division 2 – Western Conference

Wightlink Buccaneers - Player Statistics – Regular Season

Player	P	G	A	Pts	PIM
Blair Dubyk	9	8	10	18	22
Ricky Attrill	9	5	1	6	10
Sean Robert Richardson	10	3	2	5	0
Andrew Mccloskey	10	1	3	4	10
Andrew Robinson	9	3	1	4	16
Kurt Nicholas Tyrrelll	9	3	1	4	2
Stephen Gosset	6	0	3	3	6
Kieran Annis	9	1	1	2	8
Mitchell Philli Brown	8	1	1	2	6
Richard Nembhard	3	1	1	2	0
Marcus Russell	10	0	2	2	2
Daniel William Shier	9	1	1	2	6
Aaron Craft	10	0	1	1	14
Joe Osborne	7	1	0	1	6
Michael Palin	9	0	1	1	32
Nathan Webb	6	1	0	1	0
Jake Bontoft	7	0	0	0	0
Harrison Brown	10	0	0	0	2
Shaun Harris	8	0	0	0	0
Corey Watkins	2	0	0	0	0

Wightlink Buccaneers - Netminder Statistics

Player	GP	TOI	SA	GA	Sv%	SO
Aaron Craft	10	59	557	54	90.31%	0

Wightlink Buccaneers

Buccaneers played two home games, drawing 5-5 with Swindon 17/9 and losing 2-4 to Bristol on 25/9 before Ryde Arena was closed by the building owners. The 2-4 win away at Swindon on 9/10 was played for normal points as it was the return match to the first home game.

The S2 cup game away at Cardiff on 29/10 was the first game to be played for double points. The two previous wins – away at Basingstoke and Swindon were applied as double points games retrospectively as there was no chance of playing a home fixture and, after that, all games were away for double points.

The Buccaneers qualified for the semi-final of the cup and played their last ever game (for now...) at Ice Arena Wales on 8th March in the semi against Peterborough Islanders. They lost 2-5, having been outshot 74 to 20 – the goals coming from Kieran Annis and Blair Dubyk .

NIHL SOUTH DIVISION 2 East – FINAL LEAGUE TABLE 2016/17

NIHL S2 East	P	W	D	L	F	A	+/-	PIM	Pts
Peterborough Islanders	20	19	1	0	128	40	88	414	39
Chelmsford Warriors	20	12	2	6	80	59	21	272	26
Invicta Mustangs	20	6	3	11	73	90	-17	431	15
London Haringey Racers	20	7	0	13	70	104	-34	425	14
Lee Valley Lions	20	6	2	12	63	85	-22	261	14
Slough Jets	20	4	4	12	67	103	-36	550	12

Top Points Scorers – 2016/17

Player	Team	GP	G	A	Pts	PIM
Nathan Pollard	Peterborough Islanders	20	20	23	43	8
Jake Luton	Invicta Mustangs	18	20	12	32	12
Deivid Cetvertak	Peterborough Islanders	15	9	22	31	24
Conor Pollard	Peterborough Islanders	19	15	16	31	4
Connor Stokes	Peterborough Islanders	17	21	9	30	26
Ross Brears	Chelmsford Warriors	16	12	17	29	14
Daniel Clayton	Haringey Racers	19	7	21	28	4
Nicholas Alley	Lee Valley Lions	17	15	11	26	36
Nathan Darmanin	Slough Jets	16	13	12	25	24
Thomas Dennis	Invicta Mustangs	18	9	16	25	46
Clint Herring	Peterborough Islanders	15	16	9	25	34

Top Netminders – 2016/17

Player	Team	GP	SA	GA	Sv%	SO
Daniel Ashley Lane	Peterborough Islanders	20	569	40	92.97%	3
Sonny Phillips	Chelmsford Warriors	8	250	18	92.80%	2
John Abbott	Invicta Mustangs	13	12	1	91.67%	0
Steven Nightingale	Haringey Racers	6	272	23	91.54%	0
Chris Douglas	Slough Jets	11	569	52	90.86%	1
George Alley	Lee Valley Lions	8	63	6	90.48%	0
Billy Cyril Cook	Chelmsford Warriors	12	394	41	89.59%	1
Matthew Passmore	Invicta Mustangs	16	729	79	89.16%	0
James Andrew	Lee Valley Lions	18	719	79	89.01%	0
Robert Warrington	Slough Jets	10	405	48	88.15%	0
Matthew Brown	Haringey Racers	11	83	10	87.95%	1
Kieran William Wyatt	Invicta Mustangs	2	69	9	86.96%	0
Aaron Mallet	Haringey Racers	13	474	65	86.29%	0
Lee Mercer	Haringey Racers	8	26	6	76.92%	0

NIHL South Division 2 – Eastern Conference

Above: Peterborough Islanders celebrate winning the South 2 League, Cup & Play Off Treble
(Photo by Tom Scott / AMO Images)

S2E Top Scorer: Islanders' Nathan Pollard   Islanders' Dan Lane was top netminder
(Both Photos by Tom Scott - AMO Images)

Chelmsford Warriors - Player Statistics – Regular Season

Player	GP	G	A	Pts	PIM
Ross Brears	16	12	17	29	14
Thomas Alexander Wilson	17	15	6	21	4
Gary Brown	18	3	10	13	16
Terry James Fillery	18	7	6	13	14
Sean Martin	16	8	5	13	18
Brandon Ayliffe	5	9	2	11	0
Jake Richard Sylvester	5	6	3	9	0
Elliot Dee Dervish	14	4	4	8	20
Donald John Campbell	17	2	4	6	26
Bailey Chittock	9	3	3	6	14
Jonathan Wicks	13	0	6	6	0
Oliver Alfie C. Baldock	2	1	4	5	4
Ricky Mills	16	2	3	5	12
Ryan James Morgan	13	1	4	5	40
Ethan Boolkah	15	2	2	4	36
Ashlee Anthony Cave	12	2	1	3	0
Brandon Jay Webster	10	2	1	3	4
George Gell	8	1	1	2	0
Samuel Nathan Jackson	17	0	2	2	2
Will Polston	12	0	2	2	20
Lewis Robery	12	0	2	2	2
Edward Alex Lay	1	0	1	1	0
Sonny Phillips	8	0	1	1	14
Daniel Paul Wright	1	0	1	1	0
Thomas Baptist	3	0	0	0	2
Billy Cyril Cook	12	0	0	0	0
Nathan Hurley	2	0	0	0	0
Abbie Jayne Sylvester	8	0	0	0	2
Richard Whiting	1	0	0	0	0
Adrian Woodyard	3	0	0	0	4

Chelmsford Warriors – Netminder Statistics

Player	GP	SA	GA	Sv%	SO
Sonny Phillips	8	250	18	92.80%	2
Billy Cyril Cook	12	394	41	89.59%	1

NIHL South Division 2 – Eastern Conference

Chelmsford Warriors 2016/17

Invicta Mustangs Team Photo by Jimmy Stedman
Back Row (l to r): Luke Thirkettle, Jake Luton, Jake Stedman, Dan Smith, Tom Mallet, James Laming, Jack Rowland, Artyom Gzribovski, Danny Terry, Charlie Schofield, Tom Denis, Kwame Holt, Jake Hurlock, Michael Stokes. Back Row (l to r): John Abbot, Carl Tyrell, Regan O'Neil, Jake Taylor, Jake Turner, Alix Deviell, Matt Passmore.

Invicta Mustangs - Player Statistics

Player	GP	G	A	Pts	PIM
Jake Luton	18	20	12	32	12
Thomas Dennis	18	9	16	25	46
Michael Stokes	16	0	18	18	8
Kwame Holt	17	8	7	15	10
Aaron Kingsbury Ferris	12	3	8	11	57
James Ross Laming	14	6	4	10	4
Danny Harry Terry	15	9	1	10	6
Jake Stedman	13	6	2	8	118
Thomas Oliver Mallett	18	2	5	7	12
Jamie Smith	5	3	3	6	16
Artyom Grzibovskis	11	3	2	5	2
Greg Hales	11	1	4	5	34
Jake Taylor	13	1	2	3	29
Alix Deviell	11	1	1	2	8
Lucy Gruber	11	0	2	2	2
Regan O'Neil	10	0	2	2	8
Charles James Schofield	11	1	1	2	33
Ashley Earll	10	0	1	1	2
Luke Thirkettle	12	0	1	1	0
Kyle Perry Tyrrell	6	0	1	1	4
John Abbott	13	0	0	0	10
Jack Hurlock	3	0	0	0	0
Stewart James Manser	1	0	0	0	0
Matthew Passmore	16	0	0	0	0
Jack Rowland	6	0	0	0	0
Daniel Smith	14	0	0	0	2
Jake Turner	9	0	0	0	0
Kieran William Wyatt	2	0	0	0	0

Invicta Mustangs – Netminder Statistics

Player	GP	SA	GA	Sv%	SO
John Abbott	13	12	1	91.67%	0
Matthew Passmore	16	729	79	89.16%	0
Kieran William Wyatt	2	69	9	86.96%	0

Lee Valley Lions - Player Statistics

Player	GP	G	A	Pts	PIM
Nicholas Alley	17	15	11	26	36
Ross Sin-Hidge	17	9	9	18	14
Chris Fox	15	8	8	16	4
James Hepburn	17	9	7	16	35
Matthew Hepburn	17	4	8	12	14
Simon Jones	19	2	10	12	6
Simon Geldart	17	3	7	10	32
Henry Aiken	18	2	7	9	22
Oliver Glover	18	3	5	8	10
Lee Hounslow	8	4	3	7	4
Ben Duffy	11	3	1	4	2
Oskar Horter	13	1	2	3	6
Robin Young	15	0	3	3	26
Matthew Eggen	3	0	1	1	2
Ben Gillingham	12	0	1	1	0
James Gosling	12	0	1	1	4
Jordan Lee Turner	7	0	1	1	4
George Alley	8	0	0	0	0
James Andrew	18	0	0	0	4
Samuel John Awoyemi	15	0	0	0	10
James Joseph	19	0	0	0	12
Ronnie Roy O'Connor	8	0	0	0	2
Daniel Tamasauskas	3	0	0	0	0
Joseph Weare	4	0	0	0	2

Lee Valley Lions – Netminder Statistics

Player	GP	SA	GA	Sv%	SO
George Alley	8	63	6	90.48%	0
James Andrew	18	719	79	89.01%	0

NIHL South Division 2 – Eastern Conference

Haringey Racers - Player Statistics

Player	GP	G	A	Pts	PIM
Daniel Clayton	19	7	21	28	4
Joshua Abbott	13	13	7	20	6
Stuart Appleby	19	5	15	20	30
Matt Brown	17	13	4	17	20
Nicholas Minhinnick	16	6	8	14	12
Ben Osborne	17	5	9	14	36
Solomon Smith	15	5	8	13	10
Robin Martinsson	17	4	7	11	6
Robert Whittleston	16	1	9	10	4
Jack Lee	6	2	7	9	97
Ryan Payne	17	2	5	7	55
Samuel Park	16	1	5	6	2
Lee Mercer	8	1	4	5	33
Elliott Davies	13	2	1	3	0
Philippe Mueller	2	2	1	3	4
Robert Veares	12	0	3	3	14
Jack Ball	18	0	2	2	26
Tomas Gilheany	12	1	1	2	8
Mark Voslinsky	16	0	2	2	2
Alistair Band	10	0	1	1	36
Matthew Brown	11	0	0	0	0
Daniil Kulakov	1	0	0	0	0
Aaron Mallet	13	0	0	0	0
Steven Nightingale	6	0	0	0	0
Chris Norris	4	0	0	0	34
David Richards	3	0	0	0	44
Andrew Rourke	11	0	0	0	0
Stuart Spence	12	0	0	0	27

Haringey Racers – Netminder Statistics

Player	GP	SA	GA	Sv%	SO
Steven Nightingale	6	272	23	91.54%	0
Matthew Brown	11	83	10	87.95%	1
Aaron Mallet	13	474	65	86.29%	0
Lee Mercer	8	26	6	76.92%	0

NIHL South Division 2 – Eastern Conference

Lee Valley Lions Team Photo by Kim Jones

Peterborough Islanders Team Photo by Tom Scott – AMO Images

Back Row (l to r): Kieron Raynor, Jack Escott, Callum Medcalf, Clint Herring, Joe Wilson, Craig Wallis, Sam Barlow, Jack Sansby, James White, Brad Wright, Nathan Long, Deivid Cetvertak, Callum Worthington Evans, James Pentecost
Front Row (l to r): Connor Stokes, Connor Hunter, Dale Jowett, Shaun Yardley, Nathan Pollard, Steve Wren (Asst Coach), Dan Lane, Steve Johnson (Head Coach), Rob McDonald, Jon Bramall, Conor Pollard, Kenny Bavin, Leon Groom

Peterborough Islanders - Player Statistics – Regular Season

Player	GP	G	A	Pts	PIM
Nathan Pollard	20	20	23	43	8
Deivid Cetvertak	15	9	22	31	24
Conor Pollard	19	15	16	31	4
Connor Stokes	17	21	9	30	26
Clint Herring	15	16	9	25	34
Shaun Yardley	13	7	13	20	18
James Pentecost	11	6	12	18	8
Kenny Bavin	19	7	10	17	6
Robert Mcdonald	20	1	15	16	18
Craig Wallis	12	5	8	13	10
Bradley Moore	6	3	7	10	24
Jonathan Brammall	18	0	9	9	16
Connor Hunter	20	3	6	9	20
Leon Groom	16	4	3	7	72
Nathan Long	14	1	6	7	0
Sam Barlow	17	4	1	5	20
Jack Sansby	18	1	4	5	22
Dale Jowett	7	2	2	4	10
Callum Medcalf	8	0	3	3	6
Callum Worthington-Evans	15	1	2	3	4
Daniel Ashley Lane	20	0	2	2	2
Kieran Raynor	9	1	1	2	26
Joe Wilson	17	0	2	2	30
Bradley Wright	17	0	2	2	6
Jack Escott	7	1	0	1	0
Taylor Romeo	2	0	1	1	0
James Antony White	5	0	1	1	0
Samuel Dean	1	0	0	0	0
Scott Robson	1	0	0	0	0
Ben Russell	1	0	0	0	0
Jake Samal	7	0	0	0	0
Thomas Henry Stubley	1	0	0	0	0
Mitchel White	4	0	0	0	0

Peterborough Islanders – Netminder Statistics

Player	GP	SA	GA	Sv%	SO
Daniel Ashley Lane	20	569	40	92.97%	3

Slough Jets - Player Statistics

Player	GP	G	A	Pts	PIM
Nathan Darmanin	16	13	12	25	24
Kirkland Rhys Evans	18	11	10	21	2
Luke Martin-Digby	14	10	9	19	4
Timo Lindgren	9	8	7	15	77
Jamie Joyce	14	5	9	14	14
Charlie Connor Dobbins	16	3	8	11	30
Cameron George Barker	11	5	4	9	8
Jack Lee	12	2	7	9	97
Harry James J. Hatfield	16	2	4	6	22
Christopher Hocquigny	17	4	2	6	10
Matt Webb	13	2	3	5	43
Jeremy Woolfe	12	0	5	5	41
Jamie Chandler	10	1	2	3	0
James Sanderson	1	1	1	2	0
Ashley Daniel West	12	2	0	2	49
Luke Joseph Dreelan	13	0	1	1	16
Mark Saunders	3	0	1	1	4
Flynn Sitch-Cunningham	9	0	1	1	6
Christopher Beal	7	0	0	0	12
Craig Cowell	9	0	0	0	89
Chris Douglas	11	0	0	0	0
Thomas Percy	5	0	0	0	0
Edward Pratt	2	0	0	0	0
Stas Prokofiev	1	0	0	0	0
Joshua A Reid	1	0	0	0	0
Adam Simpson	3	0	0	0	0
Matthew Smital	1	0	0	0	0
Robert Warrington	10	0	0	0	4

Slough Jets – Netminder Statistics

Player	GP	SA	GA	Sv%	SO
Matthew Smital	1	63	3	95.24%	0
Chris Douglas	11	569	52	90.86%	1
Robert Warrington	10	405	48	88.15%	0

NIHL South - Division 2

Peterborough Islanders celebrate their South 2 Cup final win (Photo by Oliver Hampson)

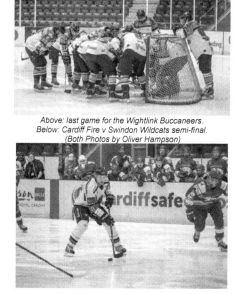

Above: last game for the Wightlink Buccaneers.
Below: Cardiff Fire v Swindon Wildcats semi-final.
(Both Photos by Oliver Hampson)

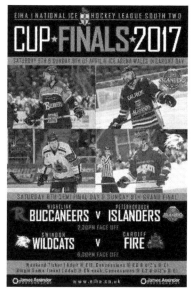

Oliver Hampson Photography

NIHL South - Division 2

South 2 Cup Finals Weekend At Ice Arena Wales, Cardiff

South Division 2 Cup Final
Sunday, 9th April, 2017
Cardiff Fire 0 – Peterborough Islanders 5
Period Scores: 0-1, 0-0, 2.1
Shots on Goal: Fire 27 – Islanders 41
Penalties In Minutes: Fire 32 – Islanders 28

Islanders Scoring: *Clint Herring 1+2, Kenny Bavin 1+1Connor Stokes, Bradley Moore & Bradley Wright 1+0, Nathan Pollard, Craig Wallis, Conor Pollard, Shaun Yardley, Deivid Cetvertak, Robert McDonald all 0+1*
Islanders netminder Dan Lane: 27 shot shut out.

Cardiff Line Up: *James Michael Whiting, Tim Burrows, Stephen Deacon, Sam Smith, Jordan Baber, Alan Armour, Jordan Powel, Christopher Hart, Tamas Elias, Daniel Self, Robert Sedlak, Andrew Davies, Luke Takel, Philip Manny, Ross Wilkinson, Samual Bryant, Jackson Lewis Price, Daniel Blakemore, Josh Elwyn Haslam, David Christian, Elis John Sheppard, David Sadler*

Islanders Line Up: *Callum Medcalf, Clint Herring, Nathan Pollard, Leon Groom, Craig Wallis, Conor Pollard, Sam Barlow, Shaun Yardley, Deivid Cetvertak, Bradley Wright, Robert McDonald, Daniel Ashley Lane, Adam Long, James Antony White, Connor Stokes, Kenny Bavin, Jonathan Brammall, Bradley Moore, Joe Wilson, Connor Hunter, Callum Worthington-Evans, James Pentecost, Nathan Long*

South Division 2 Cup Semi Final 1
Saturday, 8th April 2017 @ Ice Arena Wales, Cardiff
Peterborough Islanders 5 – Wightlink Buccaneers 2
Period Scores: 2-0, 1-0, 2-2
Shots On Goal: Islanders 74 – Buccaneers 20
Penalties In Minutes: Islanders 12 – Buccaneers 6

Islanders Scoring: *Clint Herring 3+0, Shaun Yardley 1+1, Nathan Pollard 1+0, Kenny Bavin 0+3, Craig Wallis, Conor Pollard, Bradley Moore all 0+1*

Buccaneers Scoring: *Blair Dubyk 1+1, Kieran Annis 1+0, Ricky Attrill 0+1*

Match Officials: *Andrejs Korsaks – Referee, Nathaniel Casey - Linesman*

South Division 2 Cup Semi Final 2
Saturday, 8th April 2017 @ Ice Arena Wales, Cardiff
Cardiff Fire 9 - Swindon Wildcats 5
Period Scores: 5-1, 1-2, 3-2
Shots On Goal: Fire 52 - Wildcats 38
Penalties In Minutes: Fire 52 – Wildcats 62

Fire Scoring: *Sam Smith 3+0, Jordan Powell 2+1, Tamas Elias 2+0, Robert Sedlak & Josh Haslam both 1+0, Samual Bryant 0+3, Ross Wilkinson 0+2, Elis Sheppard 0+2, Stephen Deacon, Alan Armour, Christopher Hart, Philip Manny, Jackson Lewis Price, Daniel Blakemore, David Christian, David Sadler all 0+1*

Wildcats Scoring: *Floyd Taylor 2+0, Adam Coakley & Stuart Widdows both 1+0, Toms Rutkis 1+3, Adam Finlinson, Ben Nethersell & Dan Sullivan 0+1*

Match Officials: *Sam Pering - Referee, Andrejs Korsaks – Linesman, Andrew Jarvie - Linesman*

Qualifying Groups

Group A	P	W	D	L	+/-	Pts	Group B	P	W	D	L	+/-	Pts
Cardiff Fire	5	4	1	0	16	11*	Peterborough Islanders	6	5	0	1	25	10
Wightlink Buccs	3	1	1	1	0	6*	Swindon Wildcats	6	3	1	2	-7	7
Slough Jets	5	0	3	2	-10	4*	Bristol Pitbulls	6	3	1	2	5	7
Haringey Racers	5	1	1	3	-6	3	Lee Valley Lions	6	0	0	6	-23	0

Note: Slough Jets v Wightlink Buccaneers, 28th March 2017 – not played awarded 1 point each

NIHL South - Division 2

Play Off Final – Islanders' Captain Robert McDonald receives the South 2 Play Off Trophy after the second leg at Peterborough (Photo by Tom Scott / AMO images)

South 2 East / West Play Offs

The NIHL South Division 2 Playoffs saw the top teams in the Western Conference go against the runners up side in the Eastern Conference in a home and away aggregate match to see who would advance to the two legged final. Likewise, the top finishing team in the Eastern Conference was to go up against the runners up in the Western Conference.

NIHL South Division 2 Play Offs – Final

1st Leg – 22nd April 2017	2nd Leg – 23rd April 2017	Aggregate Score
Warriors 1 – Islanders 9	Islanders 4 – Warriors 5	Islanders win 13-6

NIHL South Division 2 Play Offs – Semi Finals

1st Leg – 15th April 2017	2nd Leg – 16th April 2017	Aggregate Score
Pitbulls 1 – Islanders 4	Islanders 10 – Pitbulls 5	Islanders win 14-6
One off game at Cardiff due to no ice available at Chelmsford	Fire 2 – Warriors 6	Warriors win 6-2

Women's Hockey Round Up

Solihull Vixens celebrate with the WEL Playoff Trophy at iceSheffield (Photo by My Team Photo.com)
Back Row (left to right) : Martina Krupkova, Holly Darkins, Amy Trueman, Deborah Warwick, Rebecca Speckman, Anna Doherty, Lucy Lickman, Katerina Lossnitzer, Mariah Spare, Carol Waite.   Front Row (l to r); Elizabeth Hayward, Paige Dance, Cloë Keijzer, Saffron Allen, Katie Henry, Paige Henry, Hannah Maurice, Michelle Franklin

Above: Milton Keynes Falcon celebrate their WPL Play Off win over Streatham Storm
(Photo by My Team Photo – www.myteamphoto.com)

Bracknell Queen Bees won the WEL title for the second time in a row – their 6th league title in 6 years.
(Photo by Queen Bees).

Streatham Storm won the WPL title and promotion to the WEL for the 2017/18 season.
(Photo by Streatham Storm)

Women's Hockey Round Up

EIHA Women's Elite League
Final Table - Season 2016/17

Team	GP	W	D	L	F	A	+/-	PIM	Pts
Bracknell Queen Bees	20	16	2	2	92	22	70	98	34
Solihull Vixens	20	14	3	3	84	43	41	170	31
Guildford Lightning	20	10	4	6	77	50	27	122	24
Kingston Diamonds	20	7	3	10	52	66	-14	269	17
Sheffield Shadows	20	5	2	13	39	77	-38	182	12
Swindon Topcats	20	0	2	18	8	94	-86	105	2

EIHA WEL – Top Points Scorers 2016/17

Player	Team	GP	G	A	Pts	PIM
Natalie Aldridge	Bracknell Queen Bees	18	7	26	33	2
Christine Newman	Bracknell Queen Bees	17	20	11	31	14
Katie Henry	Solihull Vixens	19	18	10	28	26
Saffron Fern Allen	Solihull Vixens	18	11	16	27	2
Louise Adams	Guildford Lightning	18	15	11	26	6
Leanne Ganney	Bracknell Queen Bees	13	17	9	26	2
Shannon Rae Jones	Kingston Diamonds	16	18	8	26	111
Cloe Keijzer	Solihull Vixens	18	14	11	25	36
Jordan Wilshire	Guildford Lightning	17	12	11	23	20
Amy Mansbridge	Guildford Lightning	19	8	12	20	6
Jodie-Leigh Bloom	Sheffield Shadows	18	13	6	19	8
Paige Henry	Solihull Vixens	12	6	11	17	4

WEL – Top Netminders 2016/17

Netminder	Team	GP	SA	GA	Sv%	SO
Ruth Cattell	Sheffield Shadows	1	60	3	95.00%	0
Courtney Jade Newitt	Swindon Topcats	9	19	1	94.74%	0
Samantha Bonathan	Bracknell Queen Bees	18	282	18	93.62%	6
Michelle Franklin	Solihull Vixens	18	505	37	92.67%	2
Phoebe Shavelar	Guildford Lightning	14	162	12	92.59%	2
Holly Louise Steeples	Kingston Diamonds	15	572	48	91.61%	2
Rachel Moore	Swindon Topcats	19	612	54	91.18%	0
Lauren Relf	Bracknell Queen Bees	15	45	4	91.11%	3
Samantha Bolwell	Sheffield Shadows	9	292	26	91.10%	2
Gemma Bryony Davies	Swindon Topcats	8	402	39	90.30%	0
Alexandra Barrow	Guildford Lightning	20	378	38	89.95%	2
Maisie Elizabeth Gilbert	Sheffield Shadows	6	303	32	89.44%	0
Tamara Donaghue	Sheffield Shadows	2	79	9	88.61%	1
Tamara Donaghue	Kingston Diamonds	1	79	9	88.61%	1
Jessica Charlot Kinghorn	Solihull Vixens	1	43	5	88.37%	0
Charlotte Cook	Kingston Diamonds	3	118	17	85.59%	0

Women's Hockey Round Up

EIHA Women's Premier League
Final Table - Season 2016/17

Team	GP	W	D	L	GF	GA	+/-	PIM	Pts
Streatham Storm	12	9	2	1	92	23	69	96	20
Chelmsford Cobras	12	7	3	2	58	49	9	74	17
Milton Keynes Falcons	12	6	4	2	57	30	27	102	16
Widnes Wild Women	12	5	2	5	45	45	0	136	12
Slough Phantoms	12	5	2	5	43	60	-17	65	12
Kingston Diamonds	12	2	0	10	27	44	-17	225	4
Nottingham Vipers	12	1	1	10	24	95	-71	48	3

EIHA WPL Leading Scorers – Season 2016/17

Player	Team	GP	G	A	Pts	PIM
Rachel Piotrowski	MK Falcons	11	24	7	31	12
Bethany Ruth May Hill	Chelmsford Cobras	10	18	5	23	6
Nicola Bicknell	Slough Phantoms	11	10	12	22	6
Jennifer Bolton	Chelmsford Cobras	12	12	10	22	4
Carolyn Scott	Streatham Storm	10	13	8	21	12
Amy Hadden	Slough Phantoms	10	15	4	19	4
Danielle Hogan	Streatham Storm	12	7	12	19	0
Fiona King	Streatham Storm	11	14	4	18	0
Joanna Li How Cheong	Streatham Storm	11	8	10	18	2
Tereza Plankova	Chelmsford Cobras	11	9	8	17	28
Elizabeth Archer	MK Falcons	11	6	10	16	22
Leen De Decker	Widnes Wild Women	11	11	5	16	2
Katie Hills	Widnes Wild Women	10	9	6	15	28
Melissa Reidelberger	Streatham Storm	11	7	8	15	0

EIHA WPL – Top Netminders 2016/17

Netminder	Team	GP	SA	GA	Sv%	SO
Lucy Jarvis	Chelmsford Cobras	7	23	1	95.65%	0
Tegan Jenna Lavery	Widnes Wild Women	1	39	2	94.87%	0
Michaela Walker	Slough Phantoms	6	145	10	93.10%	1
Emma Bevan	Widnes Wild Women	2	71	5	92.96%	0
Kayliegh Doyle	MK Falcons	12	367	30	91.83%	2
Ruth Cattell	Streatham Storm	12	265	23	91.32%	1
Katherine Robinson	Slough Phantoms	1	34	3	91.18%	0
Charlotte Cook	Kingston Diamonds	12	484	44	90.91%	0
Stephanie Drinkwater	Widnes Wild Women	7	254	26	89.76%	0
Sarah Gunstone	Slough Phantoms	7	330	38	88.48%	0
Rachel Fairbairn	Widnes Wild Women	7	84	12	85.71%	0
Cherry Hambelton	Chelmsford Cobras	11	334	48	85.63%	0
Summer Cramer	Nottingham Vipers	10	505	74	85.35%	0
Ruth Palmer	Nottingham Vipers	3	139	21	84.89%	0
Heidi-Jane Radburn	Slough Phantoms	1	44	9	79.55%	0

Women's Hockey Round Up

Women's National League Division 1 2016/17

Division 1 North	P	W	D	L	F	A	+/-	PIM	Pts
Billingham Wildcats	10	9	0	1	89	16	73	82	16*
Telford Wrekin Raiders	10	7	1	2	52	31	21	44	15
Coventry Phoenix	10	6	1	3	26	22	4	102	13
Solway Sharks Ladies	10	3	0	7	20	47	-27	54	6
Blackburn Thunder	10	2	1	7	18	38	-20	44	5
Sheffield Shadows	10	1	1	8	22	73	-51	114	1*

Division 1 North Top Points Scorers 2016/17		GP	G	A	Pts	PIM
Leanne Clark	Billingham Wildcats	8	15	11	26	0
Rachel Serrell	Billingham Wildcats	8	10	15	25	4
Joy Craighead	Billingham Wildcats	8	14	9	23	2
Jenny Hehir	Billingham Wildcats	8	6	16	22	2
Michelle Madziak	Telford Wrekin Raiders	8	12	9	21	4

Division 1 North Top Netminders 2016/17		GP	SA	GA	Sv%	SO
Elise Valmars. Valjaots	Solway Sharks Ladies	7	288	18	93.75%	1
Megan Quigley	Billingham Wildcats	8	168	11	93.45%	1
Tamara Donaghue	Coventry Phoenix	9	312	22	92.95%	1
Jessica Sheasby	Blackburn Thunder	9	26	2	92.31%	0
Tegan Jenna Lavery	Blackburn Thunder	8	310	30	90.32%	0

Division 1 South	P	W	D	L	F	A	+/-	PIM	Pts
Bracknell Firebees	12	10	1	1	72	15	57	34	21
Basingstoke Bison Ladies	12	8	1	3	51	29	22	73	17
Cardiff Comets	12	7	2	3	43	24	19	42	16
Streatham Storm	12	4	4	4	62	40	22	75	12
Solent Amazons	12	5	0	7	37	46	-9	85	10
Oxford City Midnight Stars	12	2	2	8	22	55	-33	34	6
Peterborough Penguins	12	1	0	11	21	99	-78	36	2

Division 1 South – Top Points Scorers 2016/17		GP	G	A	Pts	PIM
Chelsea Meaney	Streatham Storm	11	23	11	34	12
Louise Beresford	Bracknell Firebees	11	18	7	25	4
Peri Edmiston	Basingstoke Bison Ladies	12	16	6	22	8
Margeurite Laffitte	Bracknell Firebees	9	10	9	19	2
Samantha Phillips	Bracknell Firebees	10	14	5	19	0

Division 1 South – Top Netminders 2016/17		GP	SA	GA	Sa%	SO
Gemma Bryony Davies	Cardiff Comets	11	227	13	94.27%	5
Meryia Throop	Bracknell Firebees	11	68	4	94.12%	4
Geraldine Park	Basingstoke Bison Ladies	11	141	11	92.20%	3
Stephanie Wicken	Streatham Storm	12	383	30	92.17%	2
Courtney Jade Newitt	Cardiff Comets	6	117	10	91.45%	2
Lauren Relf	Bracknell Firebees	8	96	11	88.54%	2

Above: Bracknell Firebees celebrate winning the Division 1 Play Off Final against Basingstoke
(Photo by My Team Photo – www.myteamphoto.com)

EIHA Women's Trophy Weekend

Women's Elite League Play Off Final – Played at iceSheffield, 4th June 2017	
For the Bill Britton Trophy	
Solihull Vixens 4 – Bracknell Queen Bees 3	

Semi Finals – Played at iceSheffield, 3rd June 2017	
Bracknell Q/Bees 3 - Kingston Diamonds 2	Solihull Vixens 7 v Guildford Lightning 1

Women's Premier League Play Off Final – Played at iceSheffield, 4th June 2017	
Milton Keynes Falcons 3 – Streatham Storm 1	

Semi Finals – Played at iceSheffield, 3rd June 2017	
Streatham Storm 6 - Widnes Wild Women 6-1	Chelmsford Cobras 1 – M/Keynes Falcons 6

Women's Division 1 Play Off Final – Played at iceSheffield, 4th June 2017	
Bracknell Firebees 6 – Basingstoke Bison Ladies 2	
Firebees win promotion to the Women's Premiere League for the 2017/18 season	

Semi Finals – Played at iceSheffield, 3rd June 2017	
Wrekin Raiders 2 - Basingstoke Bison 3	Bracknell Firebees 2 - Coventry Phoenix 0

Under 16 Play Off Final – Played at iceSheffield, 4th June 2017	
Bracknell Ice Bees 2 – Sheffield Shadows 1	

Scottish National League

Paisley Pirates secured the SNL title after a 0-6 win away at Dundee Comets in the last game of the season.
Photo by Al Goold. (www.algooldphoto.com)

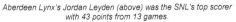

Aberdeen Lynx's Jordan Leyden (above) was the SNL's top scorer with 43 points from 13 games.

Lynx's Craig Chalmers (top right) was top netminder on Save% but Paisley's Graeme Meechan (bottom right) had a better GAA. (All Photos by Ferguson Photography)

SCOTTISH NATIONAL LEAGUE – FINAL TABLE 2016/17

SNL Table	P	W	D	L	F	A	+/-	Pts
Paisley Pirates	16	12	1	3	104	30	74	27
Aberdeen Lynx	16	11	1	4	98	40	58	26
Dundee Comets	16	11	3	2	81	43	38	24
Kirkcaldy Kestrels	16	9	6	1	86	56	30	19
Edinburgh Capitals	16	6	7	3	56	67	-11	15
Elgin Typhoons	16	6	10	0	53	80	-27	12
Dundee Tigers	16	4	9	3	50	64	-14	11
North Ayrshire Wild	15	2	11	2	29	90	-61	6
Kilmarnock Storm	15	1	14	0	36	123	-87	2

Top Points Scorers – 2016/17

Player	Team	GP	G	A	Pts	PIM
JORDAN LEYDEN	Aberdeen Lynx	13	22	21	43	6
CHRIS WILSON	Paisley Pirates	15	11	23	34	6
MARK LAING	Aberdeen Lynx	15	11	21	32	43
JOHN DOLAN	Dundee Comets	9	13	17	30	8
LEWIS GOLD	Dundee Comets	15	14	15	29	4
DAVID ORR	Paisley Pirates	12	10	18	28	16
STUART MILLER	Paisley Pirates	14	13	14	27	20
CONOR DUNCAN	Kirkcaldy Kestrels	14	17	9	26	8
JONATHON HOGAN	Aberdeen Lynx	10	12	13	25	10
GRANT REEKIE	Dundee Tigers	15	11	14	25	14

Top Netminders – 2016/17

Player Name	Team	GP	SOG	GA	Mins	Sv%	GA.Av
CRAIG CHALMERS	Aberdeen Lynx	16	431	40	930	90.72	1.94
ANDREW LITTLE	Kirkcaldy Kestrels	15	381	52	795	86.35	2.94
GRAEME MEECHAN	Paisley Pirates	15	303	26	780	91.42	1.5
MATTHEW MICHIE	Dundee Comets	16	311	32	761	89.71	1.89
CRAIG MALLINSON	Edinburgh Capitals	14	220	42	727	80.91	2.6
SCOTT BLACKWELL	Kilmarnock Storm	11	426	84	580	80.28	6.52
MARK McGILL	Dundee Tigers	10	175	24	455	86.29	2.37
ROBBIE BALFOUR	Dundee Tigers	10	259	36	445	86.1	3.64
CRAIG JOHNSTONE	Moray Typhoons	7	277	22	420	92.06	2.36
JOE BEALING	North Ayrshire Wild	9	143	30	400	79.02	3.38

Scottish National League

Dundee Comets celebrate winning the SNL Play Off and Scottish Cup double after their victory over league champions Paisley Pirates at the Fife Ice Arena in Kirkcaldy.

Scottish Cup Final - Played at Kirkcaldy: 23rd April 2017			
Paisley Pirates 5 – Dundee Comets 9			

Semi Finals			
Dundee Tigers 4 – Dundee Comets 12 (3-7, 5-1)		Paisley Pirates 26 – Kilmarnock Storm 3 (2-11, 15-1)	

Second Round - Played Various Dates			
Paisley Pirates 9 Aberdeen Lynx 4 (2-3, 6-2)	Kilmarnock Storm 9 North Ayr 8 (5-6, 2-4)	Kirkcaldy Kestrels 6 Dundee Tigers 7 (5-1,3-7)	Dundee Comets 13 Elgin Typhoons 3 (10-2, 1-3)

Preliminary Tie - Played 29th Sept & 23rd October 2016: Edinburgh Capitals 4 – Aberdeen Lynx 15 (1-14, 3-1)

SNL Play Off Final – Played at Kirkcaldy, 9th April 2017			
Paisley Pirates 3 – Dundee Comets 4			

Semi Finals – Played at Kirkcaldy, 8th April 2017			
Paisley Pirates 2 – Kirkcaldy Kestrels 2 *Paisley win on Penalty Shots*		Dundee Comets 4 – Aberdeen Lynx1	

Quarter Finals - Played Various Dates			
1st v 8th: Paisley Pirates 17 North Ayr Wild 2 (1-9, 8-1)	4th v 5th: Kirkcaldy Kestrels10 Edinburgh Capitals 8 (5-5, 3-5)	3rd v 6th: Dundee Comets 11 Elgin Typhoons 5 (7-2,3-4)	2nd v 7th: Aberdeen Lynx 8 Dundee Tigers 8 (7-3, 5-1) *Aberdeen win on PS*

British Para Ice Hockey League

The Kingston Kestrels team receive the league trophy (Photo by Paul Woollias).
Left to right: Dave Blakeston, James Ian Houliston (laying at front), Matt Woollias, Sam Fitzgerald, Tony King.
James Morris, Matt Clarkson, Stephen Gibson, Simon Berry (Player Coach)

British Para Ice Hockey Play Offs (Played at Hull Arena)

Play Off Final
Sunday, 3rd September 2017
Cardiff Huskies 0 – Manchester Mayhem 5
Period Scores: 0-0, 0-3, 0-2
Shots on Goal: Cardiff 10 – Manchester 10
Penalties in Minutes: Cardiff – Manchester 2
Manchester Scoring: Karl Nicholson 4+0, Anthony Booth 1+2
Manchester Netminder Dougy Hankinson: 10-shot shut out

Cardiff Line-up: Russell Willey, Stephen Thomas, Paul Furber, Andy Swinfen, Chris Smart, Susan cook, Tyler Christopher

Manchester Line-up: Steve Midgehall, Karl Nicholson, Graham Wilson, Pat Bailey, Anthony Booth, Rob Allen, Steve Bradley, Dougy Hankinson, Dean Lahan

Match Officials for all 4 games: Wayne Jenkins & Andrew Parker
Off Ice Officials: Richard Barker, Dave Parker, Ken Thornton, Andy Cooper, Jennie Parker, Donna Moors, Donna Hendey, Ian Houliston

3rd / 4th Place Game
Sunday, 3rd September 2017
Sheffield Steelkings 0 – Kingston Kestrels 9
Period Scores: 0-3, 0-3, 0-3
Shots on Goal: Sheffield 5 – Kingston 33
Penalties in Minutes: Sheffield 0 – Kingston 2
Kingston Scoring: Matt Clarkson 5+3, Matt Woollias 3+4, Simon Berry 1+2, Tony King 0+1
Kingston Netminder: Ian Houliston shut out (5 shots)

Sheffield Line-up: Mark Briggs, Rachel Paget, Jake Oakley, Wayne Plummer Rachel Rawson, Mark Colquitt, Gavin Dobson, Caroline Bonner, Barry Grayson

Kingston Line-up: Ian Houliston, Simon berry, Sam Fitzgerald, Matt Woollias, Matt Clarkson, Dave Blackeston, Tony King, Steve Gibson, James Birchnall, James Morris

Play Off Semi Finals - Saturday 2nd September 2017

Sheffield Steelkings 1 - Cardiff Huskies 7
Period Scores: 1-3, 0-3, 0-1
Shots on Goals: Sheffield 20 – Cardiff 13
Penalties: Sheffield 0 – Cardiff 2

Sheffield Scoring: Jake Oakley 1+0
Cardiff Scoring: Tyler Christopher 4+2, Paul Furber 2+2,
Stephen Thomas 1+2, Chris Smart 0+1

Kingston Kestrels 2 - Manchester Mayhem 3
Period Scores: 1-1, 1-1, 1-0
Penalties: Kingston 4 – Manchester 2

Kingston Scoring: Matt Clarkson 2+0, Matt Woollias 0+1
Manchester Scoring: Karl Nicholson 3+0, Anthony Booth & Rob
Allen 0+2, B Bailey 0+1

British Para Ice Hockey League – Final Table 2017

Team	P	W	OTL	L	GF	GA	Pts
Kingston Kestrels	8	8	0	0	47	19	24
Cardiff Huskies	8	5	0	3	38	33	15
Sheffield Steelkings	8	3	1	4	32	30	10
Manchester Mayhem	8	3	0	5	29	47	9
Peterborough Phantoms	8	1	2	5	15	32	5

Top Points Scorers (League Games Only)

Player	Team	GP	G	A	Pts	PIM
Matt Clarkson	Kingston Kestrels	8	29	3	32	2
Tyler Christopher	Cardiff Huskies	7	23	7	30	4
Matthew Woollias	Kingston Kestrels	8	10	18	28	2
Gary Farmer	Sheffield Steelkings	7	21	6	27	2
Karl Nicholson	Manchester Mayhem	8	14	9	23	18
Anthony Booth	Manchester Mayhem	8	14	9	23	0
Paul Furber	Cardiff Huskies	8	6	9	15	0
Simon Berry	Kingston Kestrels	10	6	9	15	2

Cardiff Huskies

No	First	Last	League						Play-Offs				
			Pd	G	A	Pts	PiM	Pd	G	A	Pts	PiM
3	Susan	Cook	1					2	0	0	0	0
4	Hannah	Farmer	3	1				0	0	0	0	0
9	Tyler	Christopher	7	23	7	30	4	2	4	2	6	0
22	Paul	Furber	8	6	9	15		2	2	2	4	0
23	Josh	Campbell	7		5	5		0	0	0	0	0
28	Jonathan	LeGalloudec	1		1	1		0	0	0	0	0
29	Andrew	Swinfen	7	1	1	2	4	2	0	0	0	0
36	Chris	Smart	6		1	1		2	0	1	1	0
63	Russell	Willey	8			0		2	0	0	0	0
71	Jason	Solman	8	1	3	4		0	0	0	0	0
77	Stephen	Thomas	8	5	6	11	6	2	1	2	3	2

Kingston Kestrels

No	First	Last	League						Play-Offs				
			Pd	G	A	Pts	PiM	Pd	G	A	Pts	PiM
0	James	Birchnall	3			0		2	0	0	0	0
4	Matthew	Woollias	8	10	18	28	2	2	3	5	8	0
5	Matt	Clarkson	8	29	3	32	4	2	7	3	10	4
8	Sam	Fitzgerald	5	2	1	3		2	0	0	0	0
10	Simon	Berry	10	6	9	15	2	2	1	2	3	2
17	Stephen	Gibson	6			0		2	0	0	0	0
18	James	Morris	5	1		1		2	0	0	0	0
20	Anthony	Martin	3			0		0	0	0	0	0
22	David	Parker	2		1	1		0	0	0	0	0
32	David	Blakeston	3		1	1		2	0	0	0	0
33	Tony	King	10			0		2	0	1	1	0
55	Ian	Houliston	7			0		2	0	0	0	0

British Para Ice Hockey League

Manchester Mayhem

No	First	Last	League					Play-Offs				
			Pd	G	A	Pts	PiM	Pd	G	A	Pts	PiM
1	Dougy	Hankinson	6			0		1	0	0	0	0
6	Karlos	Nicholson	8	14	9	23	18	2	7	0	7	2
9	Graham	Wilson	7	2	2	4	2	2	0	0	0	0
10	Pat	Bailey	3	1	2	3	2	2	0	1	1	0
13	Dean	Lahan	5			0		1	0	0	0	0
14	Anthony	Booth	8	11	12	23		2	1	4	5	2
16	Robert	Allen	4		6	6		2	0	2	2	0
17	Liz	Turner	2			0		0	0	0	0	0
32	Steven	Midghall	4			0		2	0	0	0	0
41	Steven	Bradley	6		1	1		2	0	0	0	0
	Dominic	Cosgrove	0	0	0	0		0	0	0	0	0

Peterborough Phantoms

No	First	Last	League					Play-Offs				
			Pd	G	A	Pts	PiM	Pd	G	A	Pts	PiM
7	Ian	Warner	1	1		1						
8	Robin	Gaze	7			0						
10	Naomi	Adie	6			0						
11	Matthew	Coleman	7	5	1	6						
12	Scotty	Turner	7	2	3	5						
16	Graham	Kimber	7		1	1						
18	Dave	Threadgold	5			0						
22	Stuart	Perridge	8			0						
28	Daniel	Lee	6			0	4					
29	Kieran	O'Meara	6	1	3	4	4					
32	Ali	Amini	8	1		1						
46	Darren	Brown	6	5		5	2					
50	Ben	Vernon	7			0	2					
55	David	O'Meara	2			0						

Sheffield Steelkings

No	First	Last	League					Play-Offs				
			Pd	G	A	Pts	PiM	Pd	G	A	Pts	PiM
7	Caroline	Bonner	3		1	1		2	0	0	0	0
8	Rachel	Rawson	6			0		2	0	0	0	0
11	Gavin	Dobson	2			0		2	0	0	0	0
13	Gary	Farmer	7	21	6	27	2	0	0	0	0	0
15	Rosemary	Wilcockson	7		2	2		0	0	0	0	0
16	Rachel	Paget	8		2	2		2	0	0	0	0
20	Bryan	Hackworth	2			0		0	0	0	0	0
28	Mark	Colquitt	7	1		1		2	0	0	0	0
31	Wayne	Plummer	8			0		2	0	0	0	0
34	John	Oakley	8		1	1		2	0	0	0	0
40	Mark	Briggs	5	2	2	4	4	2	0	0	0	0
41	Jake	Oakley	8	3	3	6	6	2	1	0	1	0
44	David	Scivill	8			0		0	0	0	0	0
45	Katie	Austin	2			0		0	0	0	0	0
73	Ray	Buckle	5			0		0	0	0	0	0
83	Barry	Grayson	7	4	2	6	14	2	0	0	0	0

Cardiff Huskies Team Photo

From Right to Left: Jason Salmon, Paul Furber, Josh Campbell, Andrew Swinfen, Jonathon Le Galloudec, Stephen Thomas, Russell Willey, Tyler Christopher, Chris Smart. Standing behind is coach Andy Brown

Manchester Mayhem – Play Off Winning Team

Back row: Graham Wilson, Dean Lahan, Will Main, Peter Hagan (Coach) / Front row: Anthony Booth (Alternate Captain), Pat Bailey, Doug Hankinson, Karl Nicholson (Captain), Steve Bradley / Lying down: Rob Allen (Alternate Captain) / Missing From Photo: Steve Midghall, Dom Cosgrove, Elizabeth Turner, Darren Pomfrett, Peter Bradbury (Club Media Rep), Lauren Freeman (Club Photographer)

British Para Ice Hockey League

Peterborough Phantoms Team Photo by Zara Tivey

In photo: Naomi Adie, Matt Coleman, Dave Threadgold, Robin Graze, Stuart Perridge, Graham Kimber, Kieran O'Meara, Scotty Turner, Ali Amini, Ben Vernon, Giz Lee, Ian Offers (coach) Darren Brown.

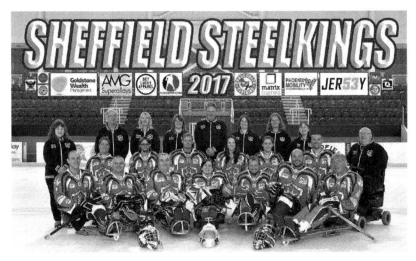

Sheffield Steelkings Team Photo by Jake Oakley

Back row (Blue Jackets) Left to right: Pete Frith, Anne Fotheringham, Beth Scivill, Peter Best, Julie Scivill, Kate Woodcock, Tracey Best

Middle row (Blue jackets at each end grey jerseys in the middle) Left to right: Elizabeth Best, Bryan Hackworth, Wayne Plummer, Raymond Buckle, Rachel Paget, Katie Austin, Jake Oakley, Stephen Smythe

Front Row (all grey jerseys) Left to right: Gary Farmer, David Scivill, Barry Grayson, Rachel Rawson, Mark Colquitt, Mark Briggs, John Oakley

WHAT HAPPENED NEXT... !

End of the EPL, more teams in NIHL North, one or two conferences in NIHL South…. Paul Breeze tries to explain….

By the time you read this, the 2017/18 season will be well and truly underway with a lot of teams in different leagues - and a few new teams around as well but, for the benefit of posterity, it is probably worth recording in print how the current / new situation came about.

In January 2017, the Manchester Phoenix EPL team finally went bump after a nomadic season and half that had seen them play home games at Deeside, Blackpool and Widnes (you can read more about this in a separate article in this publication.)

Then, two more EPL teams – Guildford Flames and Milton Keynes Lightning - announced that they would step up to the Elite League for the 2017/18 season. This left the EPL with just 7 teams for the new season and a few questions marks over the participation of Telford Tigers – who had experienced a lot of turmoil in recent years.

Offers were made to the top teams in NIHL North and South to see who would like to move up to the next level of British ice hockey, with Blackburn and Solway in the North and Chelmsford and Invicta in the South looking the most likely candidates. To the shock of the remaining EPL teams, none of the NIHL teams wanted to step up to the higher budget division and not even dropping the number of import down to three was enough to change any minds.

In fact, it wouldn't have made much difference if the EPL teams had decided to play with 5,4,3 or even no imports at all as that was not the only issue. The EPL's insistence on playing a 54 game regular season – each team playing the other 6 times – and then cup games and play offs on top of that - meant that you couldn't just keep the same squad that had played in the NIHL due to the extra time commitments involved in mid week games and the extra training and travelling. Even ignoring the number of imports, the huge increase in budget necessary to sign new professional British players made the move a complete "no no" - even for the top NIHL teams.

The EPL were left with the choice of playing on with just 7 teams for the new season or dropping down to join the NIHL instead. In the end, EIHA Ken Taggart suggested that the remaining EPL teams should do the latter as it wasn't going to be viable to carry on the EPL without any new teams.

Sheffield Steeldogs, Hull Pirates and Telford Tigers applied to join NIHL North and Peterborough Phantoms, Swindon Wildcats, Bracknell Bees and Basingstoke Bison applied to join NIHL South. All were accepted and new league structures were set up.

Things went to go more smoothly in the north and they ended up with a ten team Division 1, comprising Solway Sharks, Billingham Stars, Blackburn Hawks, Solihull Barons, Whitley Warriors, Deeside Dragons along with the three new teams. Nottingham Lions accepted promotion from Division 2 after the teams that had finished above them declined the offer.

Division 2 was also to be extended to 10 teams, consisting of Widnes Wild, Sheffield Senators, Altrincham Aces, Hull Jets, Bradford Bulldogs and Coventry Blaze from last season - plus Sutton Sting who asked to drop down from N1 - and then three new teams in the shape of Blackburn Hawks under 25s, a Telford Tigers 2nd team and a Dragons 2nd team.

NIHL South Division 1 was bit more complicated and their meeting saw them come up with a 2-conference systems with an interlocking schedule. Now, I could write a couple of paragraphs explaining how this would work but - to be honest -it is much better explained by this wonderful graphic that the Invicta Dynamos team published:

NIHL SOUTH DIVISION 1 2017/18

NIHL SOUTH DIVISION 1
- BASINGSTOKE BISON
- BRACKNELL BEES
- CARDIFF FIRE
- CHELMSFORD CHIEFTAINS
- INVICTA DYNAMOS
- LONDON RAIDERS
- MILTON KEYNES THUNDER
- OXFORD CITY STARS
- PETERBOROUGH PHANTOMS
- SOLENT DEVILS
- STREATHAM IHC
- SWINDON WILDCATS

CONFERENCE A
- BASINGSTOKE BISON
- BRACKNELL BEES
- CARDIFF FIRE
- MILTON KEYNES THUNDER
- OXFORD CITY STARS
- SOLENT DEVILS

CONFERENCE B
- CHELMSFORD CHIEFTAINS
- INVICTA DYNAMOS
- LONDON RAIDERS
- PETERBOROUGH PHANTOMS
- STREATHAM IHC
- SWINDON WILDCATS

The NIHL South Division 1 will comprise of 12 teams divided into 2 conferences. Teams will play sides in their conference 4 times (2 at home and 2 away) for a total of 20 games. Teams will also play sides in the other conference 2 times (1 at home and 1 away) for a total of 12 games. Final league position in the NIHL South Division 1 will be determined as a result of all 32 games.

FULL DETAILS ON OUR WEBSITE - WWW.INVICTADYNAMOS.CO.UK

Everybody appeared happy with this new arrangement at first but the cracks soon began to appear.

Solent Devils – arguably the weakest of the South 1 teams realised that they wouldn't be able to cope in the new league and applied to drop to the lower budget - and single conference - South Division 2.

Oxford City Stars – fearing the financial implications of remaining in South 1 joined them as did, more surprisingly, Chelmsford Chieftains.

Needless to say, this sudden move caused a huge fuss in both leagues as it was obvious that the 2-conference South 1 could not possibly operate with three fewer teams and there followed a period of intense nervousness while discussions went on as to whether the three teams would even be allowed to join South Division 2.

South Division had originally planned to revert to a single league from the East and West conferences of the past few seasons and, with the addition of a new Cardiff Fire 2 team to replace the Fire team that had stepped up to South 1, a new Guildford 2nd team and a new Oxford 2nd team as well, looked to be in pretty good shape as it was.

In the case of Solent, it was fairly straightforward manoeuvre to switch from South 1 to South 2 but, with Chelmsford and Oxford both already having separate teams entered into the lower division, there was a lot more at stake. As it turned out, both the long standing Warriors and the fledgling Stars development team agreed to make way for their senior counterparts.

Thus the league formats that have today were finally brought about. NIHL South Division 1 became a single division with the addition of a cup competition for those teams that wanted extra games and South Division 2 remained a single division with a few different teams in it that originally expected.

Whether it will remain like that for the duration of the season - or into the following one – remains to be seen!

Manchester Phoenix EPL match at Fylde Coast Ice Arena, September 2016

TEAMS LOST 2016-2017

The period covered by the edition – Summer 2016 to Summer 2017 - was a terrible time for ice hockey clubs in the EIHA as a massive 10 teams were lost due to rink closures, financial difficulties or political infighting.

It started with the Sheffield Spartans fiasco last summer that we touched on in the 2016 NIHL Yearbook and went from bad to worse. Here's a run-down of the teams that fell by the wayside in chronological order:

Sheffield Spartans (Pre-season 2016)

Sheffield Spartans, despite being the higher ranked and more successful of the Sheffield based NIHL teams, were forced out of existence after some politically in fighting within the Sheffield ice hockey club organisation meant they couldn't get ice time for the new season. It was all the more disappointing since the Spartans had a full squad of players signed, sponsorship in place and were ready to compete for the new season.

Team captain Ollie Barron went to join Widnes Wild in North 2 as their new player coach and took several other Spartans players. A few other Spartans players joined the North 2 Senators who were the remaining Sheffield team in the NIHL.

Cardiff Devils (Pre-season 2016)

The Cardiff Devils NIHL team failed to take up their place in South 1 for the 2016/17 season after having had a disastrous camping the year before, finishing rock bottom of the league table. There had been bad blood around the Cardiff set up for a while after a new Cardiff Fire team had been set up to run the NIHL teams but then cynically denied ice time and had to put their plans on hold for a season.

However, Cardiff Fire did eventually manage to take over the Devils' South 2 spot for the 2015/16 season and won the league title at the first attempt. While the Fire team was able to attract the pick of the lower league players from Cardiff and beyond, the Devils S1 team were on a downward spiral and, while it is always a shame to lose any club at any level, this departure was far from a big surprise.

Wightlink Raiders line up for the start of what would be a very short season

Wightlink Raiders (October 2016)

Following a rocky 18 months that had seen their Ryde Arena rink threatened with closure, saved by a Fans Trust, closed due to storm damage, repaired and then reopened for business, Raiders fans will have been glad to see the team start out on the 2016/17 NIHL campaign.

However, just weeks into the new season, their hopes were dashed once again after the leaseholders of the building decided that it was not financially viable to continue running as an ice rink and promptly threw the Fans Trust out, citing outstanding rent as being owed.

The Raiders team began training at the Gosport rink and played a couple of home games there but it was expensive and difficult for Island –based fans to travel there for games and it soon became clear that it wasn't going to be practical to run a whole season on that basis. The Wightlink Raiders dropped out of the league at the end of October and their results were expunged from the records.

Wightlink Buccaneers (April 2017)

The Wightlink South 2 team were also affected by the closure of the Ryde Arena but, as they were playing in a lower budget league, they were able to carry on until the end of the season, playing their remaining games away for double points. In view of the problems that they had to overcome, a place in the cup semi-final and third place finish in the league table was a pretty good return for the season.

The Ryde Arena building is still empty and a pressure group is trying to get the council to repossess the lease off the finance company who own it but, at the time of writing – ie July 2017 – no specific plans were in place to bring ice hockey back to the Isle of Wight.

Manchester Phoenix (January 2017)

The Phoenix EPL team started off playing its home games at the Blackpool based Fylde Coast Ice Arena which turned out to be a bit of disaster as the spectator facilties were nowhere near up to EPL standards and it became increasingly difficult to operate the high budget team with a drastically reduced ticket revenues.

The team cut all their overseas players and paid British players in January to try and save money and played a couple of home games at Widnes in order to give their Manchester based fans a shorter journey to watch a home game. There were hopes that a consortium would come in with a rescue package to enable the team to carry on to the end of the season and beyond but nothing was forthcoming and the team that was originally set up to keep the ice hockey flag flying in Manchester back in 2002 was finally obliged to throw in the towel.

Blackburn Eagles celebrate the Laidler Conference League Title. (Photo by Ella Thornton - Hawk Photography)

Blackburn Eagles (April 2017)

One of the most shocking club losses came about at the end of the Laidler Conference North 2 season in NIHL North. The Blackburn Eagles had put together a very competitive team and, for the first time in their history, won silverware as they finished up champions of the Laidler Conference – and looked good to pick up the double with a win at the play off weekend as well.

However, just days after receiving the Laidler trophy, the Eagles club announced that they would not be able to play the following season and claimed they were being forced out of existence by their home arena.

An awful lot has already been written about this in the local media, various ice hockey websites and, of course, Facebook, so anybody who is particularly interested in picking apart the nitty gritty of this affair will have no trouble in finding lots of sources to refer to.

There were lots of conspiracy theories being thrown about, but the basic facts as we understand them were as follows:

- The Eagles would be required to accept promotion to the Moralee Conference for the 2017/18 season.

- The Eagles would have to accept a revised ice time / Arena usage contract that would significantly increase their costs

- AND they could NOT continue with their main team sponsor of the past two years - Totally Wicked - as the rink was going to enforce a ban all smoking and tobacco advertising in line with European regulations.

The club complained that all this had been sprung on them at the last minute with a very short deadline that did not give them time to explore new sponsorship avenues while the Arena said that the advertising ban had already been announced the year before and the Eagles just hadn't acted upon it.

The management also said that the new ice time costs would merely put the Eagles club on an even footing with the existing Hawks Moralee team, as the Eagles had previously benefited from lower rates which would be unfair if the two teams were going to be in competition with each other.

The Eagles claimed that they were being treated unfairly and would be forced out. One interesting point to mention here is that the Arena would only offer the Eagles an ice time contract to play in the Moralee Conference for the 2017/18 season and there was no option for them to remain in the, lower budget, Laidler Conference.

There were already rumours flying around that the Hawks were planning to enter their own Under 25 team in the Laidler for the new season and, with ice time and match night availability always at a premium, it is hard to see how the Arena ever imagined that they would be able to accommodate TWO teams in the Moralee Conference and one more in the Laidler alongside their extensive junior programme and women's team.

The Eagles took to the ice for the last time in the semi final of the Laidler play offs at iceSheffield on 8th April 2017. The roller-coaster of emotions of the previous weeks may well have got the better of them as they lost 1-3 to Sheffield Senators.

Haringey Racers (May 2017)

A sort of coup was mounted at the NIHL South meeting in May when it was agreed that a new team called the Haringey Huskies would be playing South 2 hockey at Alexandra Palace in place of the existing Racers team that had played for the past 4 seasons. There were claims that the Racers team owed money to the venue and both the Palace and the EIHA rubber stamped the new arrangements.

Chelmsford Warriors (May 2017)

One of the most prominent – albeit indirect – casualties of the EPL meltdown and the expansion of the NIHL to accommodate 7 extra teams were the South 2 Warriors team. They had won the league, cup and play off treble the previous 2015/16 season and were runners up in league and play offs last season as well. The club had operate since the 2007/8 season and offered an excellent bridge between the Chelmsford junior teams and the senior Chieftains side but once the Chieftains had decided that they couldn't compete financially with the other teams in the new look South 1 division and applied to drop to South 2 instead, there was, sadly, no room for the Warriors in the new set up.

Oxford S2 Development Team (May 2017)

Just as the Chelmsford Warriors were forced out of the South 2 Division by their senior side dropping down a league, the new – still very much on paper - Oxford development team went the same way when the Stars team also decided that they wouldn't be able to compete in South 1.

Telford Tigers EPL (May 2017)

The Telford Tigers were the last of the 7 remaining EPL teams to apply to join the NIHL for the new season however, what actually happened was that the previous EPL club effectively disbanded and the mantle of running Telford's ice hockey team was taken on by the organisation that had operated the Tigers NIHL team last season.

Slough Phantoms (July 2017) and Billingham Wildcats (August 2017)

During the summer, two prominent women's teams announced that they wouldn't be able to compete in the new season. Both cited the inability to attract enough players although Billingham were particularly critical of an EIHA rule which penalises teams that travel with less than the permitted number of players to fulfil a fixture under which, where even if they were to win, they would still forfeit the game 5-0 if they didn't have the requisite number of players. It was suggested that this would put teams off wanting to take part in the league and helps to undermine the recent well-meaning attempts by the EIHA to attract more girls into taking up the sport.

Bookshelf

A YEAR IN THE WILD

The 2016/17 season following Widnes Wild in the NIHL North Laidler Conference

A special souvenir booklet to celebrate Widnes Wild's first trophy win in their relatively short 4 year history, featuring match reports from all Widnes Wild games for the season and game sheet information and photos as available.

It also includes end of season stats, interviews, a review of the Wild women's team's season and much more besides.

Selling price £8.50 inc free UK P&P

On sale by mail order from www.icehockeyreview.co.uk

Fylde Flyers
A Complete Record
ISBN 978-1-909643-13-0
150 pages paperback

Selling Price: £10.00

The Seagull Has Landed
ISBN 978-1-909643-01-7
84 pages softback

Selling Price: £6

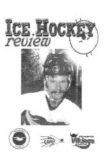

Bruce Sims
Souvenir Programme

Selling Price: £2.00

New Work in Progress! Contact us for details.
Memories of former players and fans sought for inclusion.

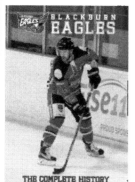

Blackburn Eagles
The Complete History

Formed in 2012 to take over from the Lancashire Raptors, the Blackburn Eagles captured the hearts of many, going from bottom of the league to champions in just 5 seasons.

The legacy will continue even though the club is no more. Read the whole story of the Blackburn Eagles.

Contents include:
Historical Background
Photos, summaries and statistics for all 5 seasons from 2012/13 to 16/17
Summary of Player Statistics
Summary of All Time League Results
A to Z Player Directory
Lancashire Raptors Players Stats Archive

Edited by Paul Breeze with Darren Shaw and Andrew Duxbury
ISBN 978-1-909643-12-3

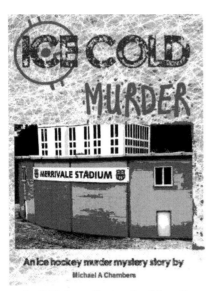

An ice hockey murder mystery story by
Michael A Chambers

Available by mail order direct from the author by sending £8.75 by

*Paypal to **spikc2004@yahoo.co.uk***

or a cheque to:
17 Robina Drive, Giltbrook, NOTTINGHAM NG16 2UX

ICE COLD MURDER
by Michael A Chambers

A murder mystery story centred around a game of Ice Hockey!

The town of Merrivale is of average size and population that contains the usual; housing and amenities it warrants and Saturday afternoons are strictly reserved for the weekly game of football, hockey and rugby as well as a shopping spree for the locals.

When a body is found within hockey owner Mark Atkin's establishment, Inspector Dilley has to unravel this terrible scene in order to find out what happened. Amongst a complexity of doors, keys and camera pictures which have much to do with it all.

Many people have much to do with the events that occur this day which puts them 'in the frame' within this much troubled club. **BUT WHO DID IT?**

23534510R00090

Printed in Poland
by Amazon Fulfillment
Poland Sp. z o.o., Wrocław